So You Want to
Write a
Children's
Book

So You Want to
Write a Children's Book

An Insider's Handbook For Children's Writers and Illustrators
Who Want to Get Published

Peter Carver

Red Deer PRESS

Published by Red Deer Press, A Fitzhenry & Whiteside Company
195 Allstate Parkway, Markham, ON, L3R 4T8
www.reddeerpress.com

Cover and text design by Daniel Choi
Cover Image Courtesy Daniel Choi
Printed and bound in Canada by Webcom

5 4 3 2 1

We acknowledge with thanks the Canada Council for the Arts, and the Ontario Arts Council for their support of our publishing program. We acknowledge the financial support of the Government of Canada through the Canada Book Fund for our publishing activities.

ONTARIO ARTS COUNCIL
CONSEIL DES ARTS DE L'ONTARIO

Canada Council   Conseil des Arts
for the Arts   du Canada

Canadian Cataloguing in Publication data is available on file from Library and Archives Canada, ISBN: 978-0-88995-456-4.

Publisher Cataloging-in-Publication Data (U.S.)
Carver, Peter.
So you want to write a children's book: an insider's handbook for children's writers and illustrators who want to get published / Peter Carver.
[136] p. : ill. ; 15.2 x 22.9 cm.
Summary: Handbook for aspiring children's authors and illustrators; a guide to the book writing and publishing process.
ISBN: 978-0-88995-456-4 (pbk.)
1. Children's literature--Technique. 2. Illustration of books. I. Title.

808.06/8 dc22 PN147.5.C3794 2011

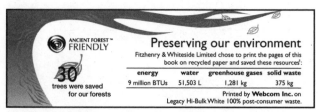

ANCIENT FOREST™
FRIENDLY

Preserving our environment

Fitzhenry & Whiteside Limited chose to print the pages of this book on recycled paper and saved these resources[1]:

energy	water	greenhouse gases	solid waste
9 million BTUs	51,503 L	1,281 kg	375 kg

30 trees were saved for our forests

Printed by **Webcom Inc.** on Legacy Hi-Bulk White 100% post-consumer waste.

[1]Estimates were made using the Environmental Defense Paper Calculator.

FSC
www.fsc.org

MIX

Paper from
responsible sources

FSC® C004071

The Earth is
degenerating
these days.
Bribery
and
corruption
abound.
Children
no longer
mind parents.
Every man
wants
to write
a book,
and
it is
evident
that the end of
the world
is
approaching
fast.

—Assyrian tablet
2800 B.C.

Contents

Preface by Caroline Pignat   1

Introduction   3

A. FOR THE WRITER

1. Getting Started   12
2. Can someone teach me how to do it?   15
3. Why are you writing for children?   19
4. Producing the manuscript   21
   What's a story?   21
   The picture book   23
   Fiction   26
   Poetry   30
   Drama   31
   Non-fiction   31
5. Completing the manuscript   35
6. Who are you writing for?   38
7. Sending the manuscript out   40
   Selecting a publisher   41
   Educational   41
   Trade   42
   Magazines   44
   Self-publishing   44
8. Commissioned, solicited, and unsolicited manuscripts   47

9. SUBMITTING THE MANUSCRIPT   49

10. WAITING FOR THE REPLY   52

11. SO YOU'RE GOING TO BE PUBLISHED   56

B. FOR THE ILLUSTRATOR

1. WORKING AS AN ILLUSTRATOR   60

2. ILLUSTRATING PICTURE BOOKS   61

3. ILLUSTRATING NON-FICTION   63

4. TRAINING AND BACKGROUND   65

5. STARTING OUT   67

6. MAKING THE APPROACH: PLANNING YOUR PORTFOLIO   69

7. GETTING HIRED   72

8. THE ILLUSTRATOR AS FREELANCER   75

C. FOR WRITERS AND ILLUSTRATORS

1. HOW A PUBLISHING HOUSE WORKS   78

2. HOW TO FIND A PUBLISHER   81

3. COPYRIGHT   83

4. HOW DO YOU GET PAID?   87

5. CONTRACTS   90

6. SHOULD YOU GET AN AGENT?   92

7. THE NEW TECHNOLOGY   94

8. ORGANIZATIONS   96

9. GOVERNMENT CULTURAL PROGRAMS AND GRANTS   106

10. RESOURCES   108

AFTERWORD   117

ACKNOWLEDGMENTS   119

INDEX   123

PREFACE

~

Everyone's got a book in them. A great idea. A funny childhood memory. A crazy dream they know would make a fantastic novel. We carry it around like a dirty little secret. Like Gollum's "precious." It consumes us as we fantasize about it, envisioning the cover face out, front and center in the bookstore. We've practiced our sloppy author signature. We already know who we'll get to do the illustrations, who we'll dedicate it to and who we'll thank in our award-winning speech. Maybe we've even started the book. Or at least bought another new journal. And some more pens. The good ones.

But something always stops us from actually writing. We feel its watchful all-seeing eye burning up every line. It's the dreaded critic. Our worst one. Ourselves.

Me, a writer? Pshhhht!

Published?! Are you kidding me?

I'll never even get this finished!

For the truth of it is, we don't even know where to begin.And so we go in circles from delusions of grandeur to the depths of denial. It's sick, really. But we can't help ourselves. We're writers. Fresh from the shire. But we don't know what we're doing.

If only some wise soul could tell us the way, give us the knowledge, help us use our creative powers for good ...

And who comes along, but Peter Carver.

Well, okay, he didn't really come along—I stalked him. I read his authors. I traveled to Toronto to hear him speak at a conference and the following summers flew to Nova Scotia for his writing retreats. But, come on, the path to publishing that first novel is daunting. Terrifying. Paralyzing. I needed answers: *Where do I get started? How do I finish? And what happens if I come upon a great clause-breathing contract?*

Teacher, author, publisher, and award-winning editor—Peter has the tools to untangle every author's frustrations. He knows the business and the art. He knows the processes. He empathizes with not only the writer but also the reader. Your readers. And yes, you will have them.

Peter has given me much wisdom and guidance over the years but I think the best advice he ever gave me was: "Your job as a writer is to write."

It sounds so simple—and it is, really. We complicate the journey with our fears and hypothetical meanderings. But under Peter's guidance, like countless other aspiring writers, I found my voice. He helped me tune in, and suddenly my stories were freed. That small seed of an idea that I'd toyed with in high-school writers craft twenty years earlier not only sprouted, it flourished into a Governor General's Award-winning series.

And with this book in your hands, you've got all you need to do the same. Learn the business, hone the craft, find your voice, and write. Write. *WRITE!*

Because I'll bet there's more than one book inside of you.

—Caroline Pignat

INTRODUCTION

~

When I was a young boy growing up in Toronto, I was blessed by being part of a family who fed their souls on good books and music and lively conversation. It is impossible for me to remember a time when books weren't part of the fabric of day-to-day life. The mesmerizing words and paintings of Beatrix Potter. *Winnie the Pooh* and his absurdly lovely view of the world. John Masefield's adventure novel for boys, *Jim Davis.* The darkly engaging *Grimm's Fairy Tales.* Marshall Saunders' *Beautiful Joe*, which taught me about compassion and cruelty, especially as it pertained to the animals in our life. The series of Sunnybank dog books by Albert Payson Terhune. Mark Twain's *Tom Sawyer*—and many more.

Curiously enough—at least in hindsight—none of these close-in favorites were books about Canada or Toronto. Though, wait a minute—*Beautiful Joe* was written by a Canadian, but the original setting of the story was shifted to Baltimore because, as we all knew, real stories couldn't happen in Canada, a kind of benign cultural wasteland—or so we

"ON THE OTHER HAND, PARENTS AND TEACHERS WHO CARE ABOUT READING WERE DEMANDING HIGH QUALITY BOOKS FOR THEIR CHILDREN."

were given to understand. The stories I grew up with came from other parts of the world. But they felt like home, familiar to me as the neighborhood I lived in, the streets of my city, the family cottage I went to each charmed summer. Perhaps the one glimpse of my own country that I enjoyed during these years was through the works of my maternal grandfather, a distinguished Canadian novelist whose pen-name was Ralph Connor and who, as Rev. Charles Gordon, had been a charismatic and eloquent Presbyterian minister in the city of Winnipeg until his death a year after I was born. In our home in Toronto, there was a shelf of Ralph Connor's books—he wrote almost thirty novels, mostly about the frontiers of Canada when the American frontier was no longer there. I remember dipping into a few of these books, notably *Glengarry School Days*, and *The Patrol of the Sun Dance Trail*, one a classic account of the early days of the Glengarry settlement in pre-Confederation Upper Canada, and the second an adventure story about the Rocky Mountains in the late nineteenth century.

"EVEN WITH THE PERENNIAL ANXIETIES ENDEMIC TO THE PUBLISHING INDUSTRY, IT IS APPARENT THAT CHILDREN'S BOOKS REMAIN A PRIORITY FOR THOSE WHO SEEK TO NURTURE AND EDUCATE YOUNG PEOPLE."

From one point of view, it didn't matter where the books I read had originated. They are still a part of me, and I cherish them. I imagine that throughout the English-speaking world, millions of children had similar experiences. In the schools of Ghana and Australia, Beatrix Potter and Enid Blyton would have been handed to young readers, and in many countries Tom Sawyer's painting of Aunt Polly's fence was an indelible part of childhood; though the flavor of Mark Twain's Mississippi is unmistakable, the roguery of Tom and his friends is about childhood anywhere.

There are lessons here for any would-be writer who wants to concentrate on the children's audience. The truths about childhood—a constant yearning to come of age, a fascination with the new and unknown, the perennial appeal of an exciting adventure, that child's eye view of the world that is lively and innocent and energetic and sometimes fearful—all are part of children's literature. And, while the earliest books aimed at the young audience appeared more than 200 years ago, the twentieth century saw a burgeoning of literature for children. Certainly by the 1980s, when I began to be aware of the children's publishing industry from working in the field, I was aware that there was an enormous surge of it around the world. On the one hand, production techniques involving ever more sophisticated computer technology resulted in ever more dazzling books for younger readers. On the other hand, parents and teachers who cared about reading were demanding high quality books for their children. Gifted authors, illustrators, designers, editors, and publishers were at work in scores of countries, responding to a demanding and competitive world market. The flood of beautiful and absorbing books for children is a phenomenon that is not limited by international boundaries or national cultures. Truly, there are always new stories to be told and old stories to be rendered in fresh and interesting packages.

Currently, it's not clear what affect electronic books will have on the children's market, but it's safe to say that material designed for young readers will somehow shape itself into a form that will be accessible through e-readers of various shapes and sizes. At the same time, it's likely that the book itself will still be with us for years to come. Even with the perennial anxieties endemic to the publishing industry, it is apparent that children's books remain a priority for those who seek to nurture and educate young people. Though consolidation and attrition has reduced the number of book publishing firms around the world, somehow a core group of children's publishers has been able to survive in the midst of the ongoing pressures of media consolidation and shifting markets.

Along with the arrival of electronic media, the arrival of the so-called "big box" bookstores has posed a challenge to publishing in a variety of markets. One consequence of that development has been the loss of a number of devoted independent booksellers who were vital supporters of quality book publishing—coupled with the loss of some fine publishing firms who have been unable to survive the rocky years of quickly changing conditions in the book trade.

It could be said that, in many countries, cultural commodities aimed at children have always taken a back seat. To distinguished critics and academics, literature for children is not usually reckoned into the mix of what is seen as a national literature. And in many countries like those that were once part of the British Empire, a native children's literature was never a priority. It was regarded as more important to stimulate a literature for adults first, to establish some sort of standard for young and emerging nations trying to find a distinct voice for themselves. It could be argued that in *The Adventures of Tom Sawyer*, children's literature in the United States got its first distinctive voice and character. In Canada, *Anne of*

Green Gables performed the same vital function—though *Anne* was not initially thought of as a story solely aimed at children. And it's probable that elsewhere in the world, similar signal stories brought into focus the demands and tastes of children as distinct from adult readers.

Interestingly, stories for children have always traveled well. From *Heidi* to *Pinocchio* to Hans Christian Andersen's fairytales to *The Jungle Book*, national barriers have meant little. A good story is a good story in whatever language or idiom. And now there are highly organized vehicles for the exchange of stories and children's culture around the world. At the annual International Children's Book Fair in Bologna, Italy, children's publishers from around the world gather to inspect and trade rights for each other's books. The International Board of Books for Young People (IBBY) has national sections in over seventy countries around the world, all promoting the importance of children's reading and literary education. IBBY's annual conference attracts writers, illustrators, editors, publishers, teachers, and librarians who meet and share their enthusiasm for books for young people. And, as more and more countries in the developing world gain the confidence needed to generate their own distinctive stories for young people, world literature for children is becoming all the richer.

It's a good time to be involved in the creation of books for young readers, in other words. It's also a very competitive time. Publishers are avid searchers of new talent, constantly on the lookout for innovative, intelligent, and witty manuscripts and artwork. The major houses, as well as the smaller high-quality publishers, are deluged with thousands of manuscripts each year.

Unfortunately, the majority of manuscripts arriving on publishers' doorsteps are ill-conceived and inappropriate for young readers. Thus the logic for this handbook.

This guide is intended to assist those entering the children's writing and illustrating community for the first time. Its aim is to help you avoid making the most glaring of mistakes, committing

> "UNFORTUNATELY, THE MAJORITY OF MANUSCRIPTS ARRIVING ON PUBLISHERS' DOORSTEPS ARE ILL-CONCEIVED AND INAPPROPRIATE FOR YOUNG READERS. THUS THE LOGIC FOR THIS HANDBOOK."

the most obvious of gaucheries. It is intended to provide you with technical pointers that might make the completion of a manuscript a less daunting task. These pages review some of the most essential requirements for those who would write and illustrate for children, and be published.

Whether you intend your writing to find the broadest possible market through a commercial publisher, or whether you want to write that perfect story for your own child, the class you teach, or the community you are part of, this guide offers encouragement, advice, and the opportunity of discovering in yourself the writer you would like to be.

A
FOR THE WRITER

...

PHILIP PULLMAN ON HOW TO WRITE A BOOK

First, make a plan. Get a large piece of paper, the largest piece you can find, and some of those little yellow Post-it notes. Write down an idea for a scene on each of the yellow stickers and stick it somewhere on the paper. When you have a whole bunch of them, say about forty or fifty, move them around till they are in the best order you can find. That's the plot.

Next, you make up some characters. You need a mixture of good ones and bad ones, old ones and young ones, rich ones and poor ones, pretty ones and ugly ones, and so on. That way every reader will have someone to identify with.

Then you need to do some research. You want to write about life in a medieval castle? Go to the library and look it up. You want to know what kind of clothes they wear in the north of Finland? Go and find a *National Geographic*. You need to do lots of research. Make photocopies of everything you need. The more research you do, the more interesting your book will be.

Then ...

Well, then you take your big piece of paper with the plot on its yellow Post-it notes, and your careful notes about the characters, and your photocopied information about castles and Finland, and you bundle it all up into a heap and you throw it all away.

Forget it.

It's useless.

And you start writing something completely different, something that you have no knowledge of, something that just came into your head, something that is utterly strange to you.

And you're seized by a fever of excitement. It's like falling in love; it's like setting out on a thrilling voyage; it's like no other joy in the world. You are possessed. You feel radiant. You give off light.

But ... there comes a time, part-way through (in my case it usually happens around page 70), when you fall out of love with it. In fact, you begin to hate it. You read it over and you are convinced that never has anyone, in the history of the world, written anything so slack and feeble. You are ashamed. You can hardly look at yourself in the mirror.

But because it's too late now to do anything else, and because you're a stubborn so-and-so, you write on grimly until you get to the end. Then you put it away and decide to be a football player or a film star or a brain surgeon instead. Anything must be easier than writing.

But after a little while you think ... no, it wasn't that bad.

And ... when I started it, I was really excited.

And ... maybe if I looked at it again, I could tinker with it and cut that bit out and maybe bring that character in a little earlier, and it might work

And you get it out and think ... hey, this is actually not bad at all.

And so you cut it, and you fiddle with it, and you change the order of this bit and that bit, until the story works. If it were a table, it would stand up without falling over, and you could put things on it and they wouldn't slide off, and from some angles it might actually look quite pretty.

That's the time to stop. You can polish a story so hard it vanishes under the gloss. I like stories (and pictures, and music) with a rough edge here and there. I like to see the brushstrokes, the kind of marks that show that a human being made this, not a machine. So stop before your work becomes slavish, and send it to a publisher, and hope your book meets the eye of an editor as wise and intelligent as you are, with just as much taste and almost as much talent.

Then you do it all again. Get a large piece of paper ...

Well, that's all I know about writing books. I've been doing it for twenty-five years, and I shall do it till I die.

—These words are reprinted with the kind permission of Philip Pullman

....

1

GETTING STARTED

~

W here do ideas come from? How do you overcome the fear of that blank sheet of paper, or that empty screen? Many of us think we would like to be writers but cringe when faced with having to prove ourselves for the first time. It's daunting to discover there are no easy ways of doing the writing. There are no real trade secrets that can make it easier for you. The only thing to do is to start and keep at it.

You may have experience as a professional writer in some other field or you may be a beginning writer. Whichever is the case, make no mistake: it is not any easier to write for children than to write for adults. There is perhaps no other kind of writing in which the need for quality is so vital—despite what you may see at supermarket check-out counters and on the bargain shelves of chain bookstores. If children are read to regularly, are encouraged to develop their own reading habit and respect for books early, they are probably going to be literate adults. But they need to be sustained by quality literature to maintain that reading habit.

"THE STARTING POINT FOR A WOULD-BE WRITER IS BEING A GOOD READER."

The starting point for a would-be writer is being a good reader.

Peter Eyvindson, a successful writer of picture books, recalls how he came to write his first story. At a summer course in children's literature he attended, the instructor gave her students the option of writing an essay on a topic about children's books—or writing a story of their own. Eyvindson, thinking he could out-smart the teacher, chose to write his own story, and it was only after completing the assignment that he realized he had read almost three hundred picture books in order to find out how to go about it.

If you want to write for children, read what they read—and keep on reading. Read the classics, and read what's being written today. Which of the classics still endure? How have tastes and styles changed since you were a child? Read Canadian, read American, read British and Australian—and read the best literature from around the world. Find a good children's librarian or bookseller to be your book-pusher, to feed you the best books available.

Find out what your own children are reading, if you are a parent. Talk to teachers and librarians to find out what appeals to children most. Browse through your nearest children's bookstore. Start building your own collection of children's titles. Read reviews in your local newspapers. Consult your local public library to find out about periodicals and journals that deal with children's books. Join or contact The Children's Book Council (CBC), the International Reading Association (IRA) in your locality, The Canadian Children's Book Center (CCBC), The Society of Children's Book Writers and Illustrators (SCBWI), the Canadian Society of Children's Authors, Illustrators, and Performers (CANSCAIP), and other organizations that support the reading, writing, and illustrating of children's books.

"IT HAS TO DO WITH THE RHYTHM OF LANGUAGE, CHOICE OF WORDS, EMPHASIS..."

As you read, you will find that the writers you enjoy are those who have a distinctive voice, a style with which you feel an affinity. Voice is one of the most difficult qualities to define or to achieve as a writer. It has to do with the rhythm of language, choice of words, emphasis—think of the distinctiveness of the voice of the person in your family who has a way with words, and think of the voice of a Brooklynite, a Newfoundlander, an Alabaman. Writers work hard to find that voice. They search to find territory they can mark out as their own, no matter what age they write for, no matter what genre they concentrate on. Notice that the best writers take risks rather than playing it safe.

Once you've laid the groundwork, once you've heard and savored the voices of other writers, you may feel ready to start. As you've read, you may have thought about what drives your favorite authors to write. Now think about what drives you. What are the stories you want to tell? What experiences formed you? What images do you want to capture and communicate? What characters do you want to fix on paper? What kind of language do you enjoy using?

You may be drawn to the voice of your favorite author, one who seems to speak your language. Don't be afraid of the influence that author has on you; rather, take advantage of it and work with it. In that way you will come to discover your own voice. As award-winning author Brian Doyle puts it: Steal if you must, but steal from the best. He stole from Dylan Thomas, Dickens, Shakespeare—the best.

Your first writing may be tentative scribbling, journaling, notes to yourself, phrases, headings, scraps of sentences, beginnings of stories or poems. In fact, these first scratchings make up your writer's notebook, and they should be preserved, filed, and expanded upon, however rough and hesitant they may seem to you at the time of writing. Those sentences and paragraphs might hold the germ of an idea or a freshly-turned phrase to which you can return weeks, months, or years later. Coming back to your notes from months or years before, you may well be struck by the perceptions you recorded, the moment you captured all in a rush. These apparent fumblings are part of the equipment of a writer.

TAKING RISKS

Take risks with your imagery. Don't rain "cats and dogs." Young readers have excellent eyes and ears for language. They appreciate freshness and originality. Use your own personal sources for your comparisons. Your own backyard. Your own kitchen. Your own street. Your own paper route. Your favorite bowl. Your mother's eyes. Take risks with the untried. Your style is as important as your plot. Fight cliché.

Hamlet famously apologizes to Laertes:

" ... I have shot mine arrow o'er the house / And hurt my brother."

A downhome image taken from a youthful accident. So simple, yet so elegant and true: I didn't mean it.

You can do this, too. Stay home. Your readers will love you for it.

—Brian Doyle

2

CAN SOMEONE TEACH ME HOW TO DO IT?

THE SOLITARY WRITER OR THE WRITER'S COURSE?

~

No one can really teach you to be a good writer, but good advice may help you find the writer in yourself by helping you find the voice in which you are most confident. Many great writers produce great work without the benefit of classes or workshops. Others have found that the judicious guidance and support of a respected mentor or writing partner has been a critical factor in achieving success. Each writer works in her own distinctive way.

Essentially, the life of a writer is a lonely one. For hours each day, for months and years, a writer is sealed away in a state of solitary confinement, searching and polishing, revising and rewriting.

For many who wish to become serious writers, finding the time to write on a regular basis poses the greatest problem. When can I find the time to write, they ask, in the midst of all the pressures and responsibilities of daily life? Some find it best to wake early and do their thousand words before dawn. Others work into the night, when the house is quiet and children asleep. Many professional writers begin their writing careers while holding down full-time jobs

"SOME FIND IT BEST TO WAKE EARLY AND DO THEIR THOUSAND WORDS BEFORE DAWN. OTHERS WORK INTO THE NIGHT, WHEN THE HOUSE IS QUIET AND CHILDREN ASLEEP."

as parents, teachers, librarians, lawyers, nurses, bartenders, waiters, or real estate agents. Somehow they find the time to lock themselves away to write on a regular basis. Alone, they struggle to find the voice, the words, the structure that gives expression to their ideas.

A starting point for many writers is keeping a journal, or a notebook for jotting down thoughts and experiences and observations about what is going on inside and around them. These days, keeping a blog or maintaining a Facebook account gets your ideas out there—possibly for comment from others. Gaining a little confidence about expressing yourself is a way of finding out that you have something to say, and that you possess the ability to say it skillfully. While writing letters is now something of an antique art, keeping up email correspondence with friends and family can be another way of demonstrating your ability with words—though one of the traps about email is that you can easily send it off without really considering accuracy or appropriateness, or making sure that it makes any kind of sense.

At some stage, many writers need the kind of support that can come from balanced criticism of a work in progress. This might be found in a small group of friends—or a single friend who is knowledgeable and who is prepared to be tough in assessing work in progress.

Support can come through a creative writing course, or workshop, or writers' group—the terminology is varied and depends on the origins of the group. Some writing courses are very specific and highly technical in their aims. Some correspondence courses make outlandish or misleading guarantees that need to be assessed carefully. (For example: "We guarantee that when you have completed our course, you will be able to submit a manuscript to a publisher." In fact, the price of the postage allows you to do that anytime.) On the other hand, the local writers' group meeting at your public library branch may be too soft to give useful critiques of your work.

Look for writing courses in the continuing education calendar of your local university or community college, in your local school board's adult night classes, or through the writer-in-residence program that may be available at your local public library. Contact the local branch of your national or regional writers' associations or organizations, who will sometimes offer workshops or conferences open to various writing genres. And, increasingly, there is a plethora of links online that can lead you to a host of writing groups: try Facebook groups, Google groups, and Yahoo groups, for example.

Be aware that there are various levels of writing workshops available to beginning and more advanced writers. In the program I have been part of, an entry-level course provides information on the range of genres in children's books, and encourages participants, through weekly assignments, to try their hand at each of these genres. The results of these exercises are workshopped weekly, and the instructor undertakes to provide, as well, personal comments on all work submitted; thus each writer is ushered gently into exposing her work to comments from others, but she also can avail herself of the expert opinions of a seasoned editor or writer sitting in the instructor's chair. In our advanced program, a much more exacting critiquing takes place, based on the assumption that by the time the writer gets to this level, she wants to have her work judged and assessed as if it were being submitted to a publisher.

If your community offers none of these formal educational opportunities, put up a notice in your local community center, grocery store, or school, trolling for like-minded people to join you in forming a group. Alternatively, there are myriad opportunities online to join writing groups of various kinds—a half hour on the Internet can tell you a great deal about whether there is one that suits you. Simply type in "online writing group", and hundreds of possibilities will appear.

If your writers' group doesn't work, it will likely disband in a short time—no one wants to give up valuable personal time on an enterprise that carries no rewards. But a strong writers' group can be an exciting and creative experience that continues for years. It can provide a forum for all the concerns

"BUT A STRONG WRITERS' GROUP CAN BE AN EXCITING AND CREATIVE EXPERIENCE THAT CONTINUES FOR YEARS."

that are important for writers, as well as a means of gaining valuable evaluations of your writing and sharpening your own critical skills. Many professional writers continue to meet with their writers' groups even though they have extensive publishing experience.

By becoming a member of a writing workshop in which your work is going to be examined and commented on, you're tacitly agreeing to have your ego battered to some extent. Finding the right milieu for this is vital. You should always feel as if being in this creative laboratory is safe for you, that the battering is no more than you bargained for. You have to accept that there is, on balance, much to be gained by having your work examined by your peers. If a workshop is led by an instructor or moderator, you'll want to check out that person's credentials and do a bit of digging to find out how others have fared in the environment he or she has created.

"YOU HAVE TO ACCEPT THAT THERE IS, ON BALANCE, MUCH TO BE GAINED BY HAVING YOUR WORK EXAMINED BY YOUR PEERS."

When I welcome writers into my advanced workshop, I underline the point that what is most important to all of us is the quality of the writing, that when one's writing is critiqued, it's not a comment on the writer but on the work. For the most part, I have found that those who have been in my workshop have bought into this understanding—though there are inevitably a few who find the ordeal of having their work judged by others simply unbearable.

3

WHY ARE YOU WRITING FOR CHILDREN?

~

If you think writing for children is easier than writing for adults, you're wrong.

If you want to write for children because you think you can teach young readers some vital life lessons, think again, because children can detect the "teacher" voice a mile away.

If you want to write for children because you think it's a quick and easy way to find a new career with a good income, please reconsider and, above all, don't quit your day job!

But if you want to write for children because you love stories, or because you like to play with language, or because there is something in your own childhood that you've never resolved, or because there's a five-year-old or twelve-year-old voice inside you that can't be silenced—well, you're probably on the right track.

A writer for children takes the child's world seriously. That means sensing what makes a child wonder and laugh and fear and love and grow. Many books for children deal with subjects that are small in scale, but large in implication. Recent examples in the picture book genre include a young pup who is learning to bark, an aboriginal view of the landing of Columbus in the New World, an account of the final days in a World War II death camp, the death of a beloved grandparent, the impact of the terrorist attacks of September 11, 2001, the achievement of Rosa Parks, and a child's frustration when Dad doesn't turn up at the

When asked what advice he could give someone who wanted to become a children's writer, Ted Staunton replied: "Become a dentist first."

hour he's supposed to take her home from school.

Stories for children can be light and entertaining, or dark and foreboding. It's a commonly accepted axiom that you can take the young reader into a dark room and turn out the light, but you must not shut the door. There must always be hope, however insubstantial and remote. Literature for children needs to be supportive, but it must never be saccharine. And literature for children can and should often be playful, but never inconsequential.

Any writer who wants to get published needs to be familiar with the children's market—with what is being published and sold now—but a children's writer should probably withstand the temptation of being sheerly market-driven. It's worth remembering that it can take anywhere from two to five years for an accepted manuscript to get published, by which time trends and styles will invariably have changed. Ideas and manuscripts that are too finely tuned to the market become quickly outdated. You are better off writing the story that matters to you, rather than spending time on a manuscript you think suits the market.

> "A WRITER FOR CHILDREN NEEDS TO POSSESS, ABOVE ALL, AN INNATE RESPECT FOR CHILDREN AND THEIR CAPACITY TO UNDERSTAND AND GROW."

A writer for children needs to possess, above all, an innate respect for children and their capacity to understand and grow. Children are capable of grasping big ideas if they are expressed clearly. That doesn't mean the language of children's books must be "dumbed down," as some cynics express it. It doesn't mean that children's books need to condescend to their audience. Sophisticated ideas and big words, as long as they are clear in their meaning and context, help young readers expand their world as well as their vocabulary. Children have an innate enjoyment in discovering new words, enlarging their language resources.

4

PRODUCING THE MANUSCRIPT

~

When we speak of books for children, we encompass a range of literary genres—picture books, novels, collections of short stories, legends and folktales, biographies, craft and activity books, information books on many subjects, poetry, drama, and others. We are also speaking of a great age range—from books for babies to novels and poetry and non-fiction for seventeen-year-olds.

Some writers work in more than one genre, while others specialize. It is sometimes hard to predict where a writer is going to end up. The aspiring picture book writer might eventually end up producing a series of craft books. A novelist might become tantalized by the challenge of producing a picture book text, or a history book. An established picture book writer might eventually produce an outstanding young adult novel. If you want to write for children, in other words, you will leave your mind open to all sorts of possibilities. A writer is a writer is a writer.

As you begin to write, you likely begin with the genre that holds the greatest immediate appeal and relevance for you, and the one that suits your emerging voice.

WHAT'S A STORY?

Story making is one of the predominant human urges. We grow up listening to stories, then reading them, and if you are entering the field of writing for children, creating stories is something you are bound to become engaged in.

What is a story? There are certain essential components—the bare bones, as it were—and here are a few of them.

A main character, or protagonist, with whom a reader can identify. The story begins when something changes in the life of the main character. And with that change there is revealed something the main character needs or lacks.

There's a problem, a challenge, a difficulty—no matter how trivial—that the protagonist has to meet and surmount before the story is complete. In a picture book story, this may not be an earth-shattering problem, but there has to be some kind of complication in the life of the main character for the reader to turn the page, to see what is going to happen next. In a novel, a steadily accumulating series of complications confront the protagonist, until at last the character has sorted out the problem and the story comes to a resolution. A story has a beginning, a middle, and an end.

> "IN A NOVEL, A STEADILY ACCUMULATING SERIES OF COMPLICATIONS CONFRONT THE PROTAGONIST, UNTIL AT LAST THE CHARACTER HAS SORTED OUT THE PROBLEM AND THE STORY COMES TO A RESOLUTION."

By the time the story has come to its resolution, the main character has grown in knowledge or strength—evidenced by the ability s/he has shown in meeting and overcoming the challenge. The main character has solved the problem; it's not been sorted out by anyone else or any other force in the story (a *deus ex machina* which miraculously appears to save the day).

A strong story has more than one plot thread. Though that may not be true in a picture book. The more layered a plot is, the more satisfying the story is, the more convincing it seems, like real life. A novel usually has at least three narrative threads, all of them relating in some way to the main character.

In a picture book story the resolution may come as a surprise (see Jules Feiffer's *Bark George*), but it will be seen as nonetheless appropriate. Often picture book plots have a cyclical nature—i.e. the character ends up back where s/he started, but with greater awareness of the world (Maurice Sendak's *Where the Wild Things Are*).

While there are many variations on the plotting of a story, these elements are common to most.

THE PICTURE BOOK

Writing a picture book may seem like the simplest task and therefore a good place to start, but in fact it can be a demanding challenge. Look closely at the picture books displayed in your local public library or bookstore, and you see they are the result of great skill and talent. The picture book writer doesn't dash off a story before breakfast and mail it to a publisher by lunchtime.

Because picture books tend to contain fewer words, each word counts for more, as it does in a poem. What's more, the young reader or listener must want to turn each page to see what comes next. The book must be built on a strong text as well as on enchanting or amusing visuals.

In fact a picture book is the product of a number of creative minds working together—writer, illustrator, art director and/or designer, and editor. Achieving perfect harmony in that partnership is an elusive goal that publishers seek but don't always attain. None of the elements should detract from the others, but each must make itself felt: tightly written text, colorful pictures that tell a story, attractively placed and suitably-sized type, and a durable package that can withstand the wear of repeated readings and handlings.

There are many types of picture books, from board books for babies, to alphabet and counting books for toddlers, to storybooks and first readers for five and six-year-olds, to longer stories for readers as old as eight or nine for whom pictures are still important. Not all picture books are stories, and not all picture books have words.

The picture book writer's job is simply to produce the text for the picture book and nothing else. As the writer, you do not have to provide illustrations of your own, nor do you have to find an illustrator for your work. While some established picture book authors are also illustrators, many more are not. Illustrating a picture book requires the kind of background and training that only comes through extensive study and practical experience (see *For the Illustrator*, p. 63).

It may be tempting, but it's wiser not to collaborate with an artistically minded friend or relative to produce an illustrated manuscript to present to a publisher. Truly professional illustrators expect and need to be paid for their time and for their finished work, and as-yet-unpublished writers should not be making that kind of financial investment—it could be in the thousands of dollars—in a project that may never be published. Also, most neophyte illustrators probably won't have sufficient experience of the publishing process to provide useful work.

Costs of producing a full-color picture book are high (in the $30,000 range). Publishers want to retain for themselves the key role of matching author with illustrator. They also decide the number of illustrations in your picture book, their size and placement on the page, etc. Publishers have the experience in this field that you do not, and the beginning writer needs to trust that the publishing house will work to produce the best possible book from the text you provide.

As you develop your picture book manuscript, you need to be aware of the technical constraints within which you're working. A picture book is usually 24 or 32 pages long—because the large sheets on which the books are printed fold into booklets (or "signatures") of eight or sixteen pages. On rare occasions, a picture book may be longer (40 or, rarely, 48), but this is considered likely to strain a younger reader's normal attention span. Once space is allotted for the title page, copyright information, and other introductory matter, the text itself probably covers between 20 to 30 pages (depending on whether the book is 24 or 32 pages in total length). That translates to from 10 to 15 double-page "spreads" available for text and illustration to tell the story.

Because of these factors, the point in the text where each page needs to be turned becomes a crucial concern for the writer—and for the designer of the book. The spreads could be seen as "mini-chapters" or distinct scenes, each with its own integrity in the developing narrative. How does your story meet these requirements? In order to find out, as you're developing the manuscript, create your own "dummy" book with the same number of pages you're aiming for in the final published book. Leave two or three pages blank for title and publishing information; then cut out and arrange your typed or handwritten text on the remainder of the pages. As you read aloud to yourself, you'll find out how the page breaks work; you may need to move blocks of text around until you achieve an arrangement that pleases you.

You will also find, invariably, that you need to edit your text, reducing the length so that the essential ideas stand out effectively. Picture book texts range in length from no words at all to just a few (as in boardbooks); to books for toddlers (less than 300 words for Kathy Stinson's *Red is Best*); to books for kindergarten kids (up to 1,000 words for Barbara Cooney's *Miss Rumphius*); to books for children in Grades 1 to 3 (2,000 words in the case of a traditional tale or legend such as the *Barefoot Tales* drawn from several cultures). But most good stories can usually be told in well under 1,000 words. Do a word count of your favorite picture book texts, just to satisfy your curiosity. One of mine is Jane Yolen's *Owl Moon*, which comes in at somewhere around 600 words.

> "YOU WILL ALSO FIND, INVARIABLY, THAT YOU NEED TO EDIT YOUR TEXT, REDUCING THE LENGTH SO THAT THE ESSENTIAL IDEAS STAND OUT EFFECTIVELY."

Producing your own dummy book, editing and revising your text—these are important steps in the creative process. Writing the first version of your text may not take long, but the rewriting and polishing and *re-thinking* process can take weeks, even months. Maurice Sendak took three years to decide on the 300 words of text for his classic picture book, *Where the Wild Things Are,* and that process preceded starting work on the illustrations.

A final point here: while using a dummy to test out your text is useful to you as you finalize the manuscript, your text should be submitted to a publisher in normal manuscript form.

Some picture book writers produce texts for books that are not stories at all. They might be alphabet books or counting books or other kinds of books that do not depend on characters and plots to propel the reader from one spread to the next. But text nevertheless needs to be carefully planned and worked out on spreads. (Note the carefully chosen 106 words in Kevin Major's *Eh? To Zed*, illustrated by Alan Daniel.)

From time to time—and it happened in the years after 2000 most recently—there has been a dip in the picture book market, and therefore a corresponding sag in publisher interest in taking on these expensive projects. Because of the cost associated with producing picture books, the publisher's investment has to be justified by eventual sales. When there are downturns in the overall book market, picture book production is often the first to be curtailed; consequently the writer looking to have work accepted by a publisher should always be aware of what's going on in the market. Ironically, despite the recent reduction in number of picture books produced, most publishers receive more unsolicited picture book manuscripts than any other genre.

FICTION

If you begin to write a picture book story—and then find it growing beyond the limits of a picture book text—you may be on the brink of composing a short story or a novel. If your characters are no longer primary level children, that too suggests an older readership—although some successful picture books are about characters who are not children, but have a child-like quality about them (for example, the riveting *Fourteen Cows for America,* by Carmen Agra Deedy with illustrations by Thomas Gonzalez).

From the very outset, you may realize that the scale and complexity of the story you want to tell requires a large canvas, one that is suited best to the novel format, which is of course much more flexible than the picture book structure.

Children enjoy having novels read to them, chapter by chapter, long before they can read themselves. *The Chronicles of Narnia,* for example, and *Charlotte's Web* have been favorite bedtime reading material for many families. Through being read to, children become accustomed to the longer story that may take several sittings to complete.

By the time they enter Grade 3, most children with an interest in reading are looking for more substantial reading material, more complex stories than they find in picture books. They are reading more on their own, and they want to immerse themselves in a world that can consume them for more than ten or fifteen minutes.

North American publishers are producing series of what are often called **"first chapter books"** or **"easy readers."** These are short novels—from less than 3,000 to 5,000 words—that children can read to themselves. For many young readers, this begins to happen around the age of seven or eight. The text for these short novels appears in easily accessible type and is often accompanied by black and white line illustrations to make the story more accessible. Some publishers have produced shorter first chapter books with full-color illustrations, a kind of amalgam of picture book and novel. Longer and more complex stories—**junior novels**—can run from 10,000 to 20,000 words, and are designed for children who want more meaty plots and involving characters. Two of the most successful books of this kind are Patricia McLachlan's remarkable novel, *Sarah, Plain and Tall,* and Kate DiCamillo's *The Miraculous Journey of Edward Tulane.* Other writers who have created such books include Julie Lawson, Ted Staunton, Chris Riddell, Lauren Baratz-Logsted, and Eric Wight.

Longer novels—sometimes called **juvenile novels** or **middle readers**—are usually aimed at readers aged nine to twelve and might run from 15,000 to 40,000 words or more, from 90 to 180 pages. Normally, they are not illustrated. David Almond's superb first novel, *Skellig*, is a good example of this level. While the early chapter book is usually contained within a few short chapters, the juvenile novel is more complex in plotting and character development and more closely resembles a full-fledged adult novel.

The **young adult** novel was conceived of by librarians and publishers looking for a level of fiction that would form a bridge between the traditional juvenile novel and adult literature. YA fiction, as it's known in the trade, began developing in the years following World War II, the outstanding prototype being J.D. Salinger's *Catcher in the Rye.* Young adult novels are designed for readers thirteen and up (junior high or high school level). It's acknowledged that young adult is currently where the action is in terms of publisher and market interest, and Laurie Halse Andersen, Kevin Brooks, S.E. Hinton, Kevin Major, William Bell, and Diana Wieler are among the scores of authors who have made YA a distinguished and ever-expanding field. The term **"young adult"** is sometimes loosely

> "THE YOUNG ADULT NOVEL WAS CONCEIVED OF BY LIBRARIANS AND PUBLISHERS LOOKING FOR A LEVEL OF FICTION THAT WOULD FORM A BRIDGE BETWEEN THE TRADITIONAL JUVENILE NOVEL AND ADULT LITERATURE."

applied to fiction for readers from ten up, but there is a growing emphasis on the older YA audience, truly the "almost adults" for whom writers like Melvyn Burgess (*Junk*) are writing edgy, gritty fiction. Some publishers are uneasy about the term "young adult," and employ the more awkward label of **teen fiction**.

Sporadically publishers have also been looking for **short stories**, which can appear in anthologies or collections, either in the form of educational texts or mass market trade paperbacks. Occasional competitions sponsored by book or magazine publishers or writers' associations provide opportunities for short story writers. As part of your research as a writer, it would be worthwhile to explore the possible markets for short fiction. It makes sense that young readers should appreciate the short story since it doesn't require the time commitment novel reading requires. A short story creates a world, introduces a set of characters, presents and resolves a problem, all in the space of a few pages, a reading time of 15 or 20 minutes. In a world where so many diversions compete for a young person's attention, short fiction is a legitimate and justifiable reading option for teenagers. And, in fact, recent short story anthologies—whether devoted to works by one author or a collection of stories by several authors—have provided some of the best reading in children's literature. The most obvious market for short stories is with educational publishers who are constantly on the lookout for short fiction to include in their reading texts for various grade levels, but there are also a number of examples of short story collections that are outside the traditional educational market. Budge Wilson's *The Leaving*, Martha Brooks' *Paradise Café and Other Stories*, Jon Scieszka's *Guys Read,* David Almond's *Click,* and Donald R. Gallo's various collections of short stories are all evidence that the short story is alive and well for young readers. There are also opportunities for short story writers in online teen zines, some of them interested in stories by teens, others in stories by adult writers for the teen audience.

Although picture books are expensive to produce and therefore require larger sales figures in order to make them financially viable, fiction is regarded as a greater financial risk for publishers. A best-selling novel may sell no more than 5,000 or 6,000 copies over a year or two, and those are regarded as good sales figures.

Yet writing a novel will likely take at least several months, or more likely one or two or three years, no matter how experienced the writer. The novelist puts in a great deal of time and effort, without any assurance that the final work will find a publisher.

The idea for a novel may percolate in a writer's mind for months or years before it finally emerges on paper. Writing it down involves knowing how a story develops, how to work out a plot, how to make characters come alive and settings seem convincing, how to use language that will draw readers into the story, how to compose a chapter so it has its own innate structure and yet also contributes to the over-arching movement of the entire story. Above all, completing a novel requires that the writer come to a profound understanding of what the story is and how it needs to be shaped and where it needs to end.

In composing any work of fiction, the writer needs to keep asking: what is the story I am telling? Some writers simply begin writing and continue, discovering the story as they go. Gradually, they realize the route the story is taking and where it will end. In the process they may have to revise earlier sections, written when they were still not sure of what the story was going to be. A writer probably has to do several drafts of a manuscript before reaching a version that is ready to be sent to a publisher.

"ABOVE ALL, COMPLETING A NOVEL REQUIRES THAT THE WRITER COMES TO A PROFOUND UNDERSTANDING OF WHAT THE STORY IS AND HOW IT NEEDS TO BE SHAPED AND WHERE IT NEEDS TO END."

Other novelists plan meticulously each step of their story, spending weeks or months getting ready to write. They map out the plot, they acquaint themselves with details of the geography of the setting, they research any specialized information that will be included in the story (dirtbikes, computer programming, sailing techniques), they check historical details, local dialects and language, and any other information that will make the story credible. They know how the story is going to end before they start writing. Above all, they get to know how their characters think, feel, and react in all situations, and are at home in the world their characters inhabit. Mystery writers in particular need to know where the story is heading as they begin to write. Norah McClintock, author of many crime novels for young readers, says that experience has taught her that it is wise to plan in advance of sitting down and beginning to write. But she knows that, inevitably, changes will occur along the way as she gets to know her characters and sees their potential.

Some authors write the crucial scenes in a novel first, and then discover how these scenes are linked together. It may be that as a writer you begin by writing the final scene, so that you know where the story is heading. Or you may write the five or six crucial events in the novel you're conceiving of, and then spend the rest of your time figuring out how to link these chapters together.

Each writer will go about the task of writing a novel in a different way. Any novel may require a number of false starts, and a good deal of experimenting, as the writer finds out what works best. Each novelist must invent a method that works for the project being undertaken. And no matter how carefully a novel is planned in advance, rewriting is fundamental to the process; the writer may go through five or seven or even fifteen drafts before the manuscript is ready for publication—even if the project began with careful planning.

And no matter how experienced the writer, no matter how many books she's written and published, each novel presents a new series of challenges and potential risks. Not every manuscript begun necessarily ends as a published book.

POETRY

Poets are like musicians; they hear language in a particularly acute way, and become expert technicians in rolling words up against each other to produce myriad effects in sound and meaning. And poetry for children must be no less thoughtfully composed than poetry for adults.

Publishers tend to be wary of submissions of poetry for children— whether it's picture book stories told in rhyme, or collections of verse aimed at older children. So many novices writing for children think that it's good enough to concoct stories in doggerel for young readers that editors and publishers wring their hands in despair at a lot of the manuscripts sent to them.

Yet poetry is being published for children, though the list of great children's poets is not a long one. Think Shel Silverstein (*Where the Sidewalk Ends*), Michael Rosen (*We're Going on a Bear Hunt*), Dennis Lee (*Alligator Pie*). Then add your own personal favorites, traditional and less so; the list keeps growing, though slowly.

Poems for children, it's important to remember, need not all be written in rhyming verse. George Swede has produced several volumes of haiku and free verse for children, and Jean Little's *Hey World, Here I Am* demonstrated that free verse can bring many rewards for young readers.

With her 1998 novel *Out of the Dust*, consisting wholly of a series of incisive short chapters all in free verse form, Karen Hesse stimulated the use of poetry in narrative that has produced a number of powerful novels in verse for young readers. Sometimes bursts of poetry are interspersed throughout the prose of a novel, and sometimes, as in Hesse's novel, the entire story is told in verse. The form allows for an intensification of voice, a distillation of action into sharp edgy or lyrical phrases, and a revelation of character that can produce undeniable emotional resonance. The challenge is that the storyteller has to write verse well.

DRAMA

Very little drama for children is published in the conventional sense. But many young people's theaters, as well as producers of family television and film, are looking for scripts for a range of ages—original material, adaptations of existing books, and edited versions of longer works.

If you are interested in writing scripts for theater, film, or television, you should contact your local children's theater or television network. Also, your regional community college may run courses in script-writing.

NON-FICTION

Non-fiction is more than just not fiction, as its practitioners are fond of pointing out. In fact the category of non-fiction includes several sub-genres of information books: history, biography, science, and activity books. If you look through the shelves of a well-stocked children's bookstore you'll see how exciting and diverse this category can be.

Many young people who find it difficult to get involved in reading fiction discover that the pursuit of information develops their reading skills quickly, because processing the information becomes so important to them. And since the curiosity of children knows few bounds, the opportunities for the non-fiction writer are particularly exciting.

Computers, dinosaurs, sports heroes, and space are just a few of the subjects that appeal to keen young minds. Environmental and science activity books are an inexhaustible source of interest for children. Craft books present lots of opportunities for rainy-day diversions. Biographies of pop singers, athletes, and other personalities have great appeal. The biographies of Anne Frank and Helen Keller, Martin Luther King and Nelson Mandela, sports figures and war heroes are a few examples of perennial favorites for young readers.

"BEFORE YOU COMPLETE A NON-FICTION MANUSCRIPT, IT IS A GOOD IDEA TO MAKE SURE YOU HAVE AN INTERESTED PUBLISHER."

In fact, the realm of non-fiction can be one of the most fascinating and creative areas for a would-be children's writer to explore, since it allows one to follow personal interests with enormous enthusiasm and in great depth. It also allows the writer to reflect that enthusiasm and knowledge in the final product. The field of non-fiction has, at various times, been the fastest-growing and most market-driven sector of the children's publishing industry—in part because of the needs of the education system for fresh and interesting material on many subjects.

Because of the keen competition in this field, writers must keep track of what is now available in their chosen subject area. This involves researching what has already been written on your topic, consulting periodical indexes, and talking to librarians, teachers, and booksellers about what is needed—and at what age level. Publishers will be impressed by new information on a subject, a fresh angle, or a different treatment.

Once you've decided on a subject that interests you enough to absorb you for several months—or a couple of years!—of your life, you should cast as wide a net as possible by brain-storming to produce the kinds of questions and topics that fall within the subject area. Once you've explored all you might cover, you need to think about the parameters of the work, to set some limits so that the eventual manuscript is of manageable length and has a definite focus.

Though non-fiction sells well, publishers receive few unsolicited proposals for non-fiction projects. This means that the concepts for most non-fiction books tend to begin with the publisher, who then hires writers to do the work. But publishers will be impressed by a well-researched, well-planned proposal for a non-fiction project.

Before you complete a non-fiction manuscript, it is a good idea to make sure you have an interested publisher. You don't want to spend months researching a subject and writing a manuscript, only to discover that no one wants to do the book, or that a potential publisher wants a manuscript that takes a very different approach than yours—or that a book on your subject has been published recently. Publishers will be very concerned about whether a particular book project can fit in with an existing series or might be the start of a new series; they are also aware of the curriculum needs at various grade levels, which influence the age level at which your book should be pitched.

Hearing Your Story

One of the things I've found very useful when writing is to read your work aloud. When you actually hear your words, it's much easier to detect repetition, flaccid word choices, sloppy pacing, wooden dialogue. Reading aloud also reminds you that your primary goal is to tell a story. Are you being a good storyteller? Are you holding the attention of your audience? Are you using your words to their greatest effect? I always read my first drafts aloud to my kids, and then again to myself when doing the final edit.

— Ken Oppel

To test a publisher's interest in a non-fiction idea, send in a proposal consisting of: a brief covering letter explaining the overall shape of the proposed book, a sample chapter demonstrating your writing skills, and a detailed outline (up to ten pages) that indicates the treatment you wish to give the subject. Remember that the publisher will judge your ability by the way in which you frame your proposal. If that proposal is accepted, you don't need to follow the outline exactly, but having a feasible plan is important to give the publisher the sense that you are able to organize a lot of material. A writer with journalistic training might find this field particularly appealing.

It is particularly important to decide the level of reader you want to appeal to in your project. Non-fiction books can be found at every age level in the spectrum, and therefore you'll have to decide where in that continuum your book is going to work best. In deciding on age level, you'll want to consult school curricula and talk with knowledgeable teacher librarians who can tell you which themes are most appropriate at which grade levels, since much of children's non-fiction is used for school projects.

More than any other book for young readers, the non-fiction book is a cooperative venture involving writer, designer, editor, and illustrator, all working together as a team. It is also a labor-intensive project from the publisher's point of view, more so than any other kind of children's book, so a strong ability to organize material and ideas is a real asset.

5

COMPLETING THE MANUSCRIPT

~

You've had a great idea, you've done your research (yes, you need to do research for writing fiction as well as non-fiction, maybe even for a picture book text), you've got your notes all ready—and now you have to start writing. The blank page, or the empty screen, faces you.

Many professional writers find this moment the most difficult of all. It sometimes helps to realize that, in making notes and getting ready, you've already sketched out some scenes, possible beginnings, perhaps even the ending. But the first draft can be hard to begin and to finish, and there is no way to avoid the work. It requires skill—and lots of dogged determination.

On certain charmed projects, however, the writing just happens, magically. Some writers talk about the first draft "writing itself," with the ideas and characters and scenes bubbling out faster than they can be written. Brian Doyle says that when you've sat at your desk for an hour and it feels like five minutes, then you know things are going well. But when you sit for five minutes and it feels like an hour, things aren't quite as sunny.

Writers talk about ways they "psych" themselves through the early stages of writing a manuscript. Sarah Ellis speaks of avoiding her desk and writing at the kitchen table, so that she can ignore the fact that she's seriously *creating* and fools herself into thinking that she is just playing at writing. Her conviction is that the act of writing is, in essence, play of the highest order, as the creator moves around all the characters in the playhouse of her imagination.

The methods you use to get yourself through these early stages

FACING WRITER'S BLOCK

Writer's block is a dreadful affliction. I once had it for so long—and so badly—that I couldn't even go near the room where my typewriter was (this was BC—before computer). Our house was neat, the ironing was up to date, and meals were regular and more interesting than they'd been in years. I felt that I was doing the useful things, the important ones, but my husband and my kids finally said that if I didn't "lighten up," they were all going to divorce me.

It was around that time that I met a wonderful old English storyteller who told me how the fire fighters and air-raid wardens in London during the Second World War would come to her coffee kiosk at the end of a terrifying night of bombing and beg her to tell them a story. Maybe that story was what did it for me. Something did. The cloud lifted, the house was messy again, the ironing piled up, meals were late and boring. But everyone was happy.

—Janet Lunn

are your own, based on what works for you. Members of your writers' group can be invaluable in buoying you up at this stage.

Writers usually find that the manuscript isn't finished until it has gone through several drafts. The first draft is just the beginning of the process: getting the ideas down in rough form, building the framework for the house. It's in the rewriting that the rooms, doors, and windows are placed, the colors and textures worked in, and the real manuscript begins to emerge. That's when the writer may realize that a favorite passage just doesn't belong at all and will have to be jettisoned (otherwise known as "killing your darlings"). That's when it might turn out that Chapter 1 is simply "throat-clearing" and the story actually begins with Chapter 2 or 3. Or that the main character is simply a pawn the writer is moving around arbitrarily without having sufficiently thought through the character's motivation.

As they set about revising their work, fiction writers ask questions about what they have set down already. In this way, problems come to light and can be solved in a more objective way. For example, what story have I told? Is there a shape to it—a beginning, middle, and end? Is it really worth telling? Will my reader find it interesting? Is there something for the reader to think about once the story is finished? Does the protagonist grow and change? What does my protagonist need? Are my other characters credible and my dialogue convincing? Does each character have a story—even though only a few elements of that story may be told in this manuscript?

Many writers find that reading the manuscript aloud reveals

problems most clearly. Even reading it aloud to yourself in an empty room gives a sense of how the language flows, how coherent the writing is. You may want to find an audience—a trusted friend, a writers' group, even a group of children in a classroom, a public library, or the local neighborhood. Children are least likely to give you detailed critical feedback—but you can learn something from the shuffling feet, the glances out the window, and the muttering of a group of kids who are getting bored. Remember that children are not critics and sympathetic friends are not editors. A writing workshop may provide more valuable critical commentary. But ultimately the manuscript belongs to the writer and, no matter how open you are to other people's opinions, you need to balance their views against your own vision of the book you are creating.

> "NO MATTER HOW OPEN YOU ARE TO OTHER PEOPLE'S OPINIONS, YOU NEED TO BALANCE THEIR VIEWS AGAINST YOUR OWN VISION OF THE BOOK YOU ARE CREATING."

Some writers want professional advice on a manuscript prior to submitting it to a publisher. You can contact the Editors' Association of Canada (EAC), the Editorial Freelancers Association (EFA), The Writers' Union of Canada (TWUC), the Canadian Society of Children's Authors, Illustrators and Performers (CANSCAIP), the Society of Children's Book Writers and Illustrators (SCBWI), the National Writers Union (NWU) (details for all can be found in the resource section), or other organizations and services that provide this kind of feedback for a fee. A few individual published authors and professional editors also offer this kind of service, but if you aren't able to make such a contact yourself, it's probably best to begin by contacting a writers' or editors' organization for names of those who might assess your project. Such an appraisal costs money, and the level of fee should be discussed before you enter into any arrangement; professional editors may charge by the hour or on a flat fee basis. Your regional writers' association may also provide this service, for a minimal fee. But remember that the evaluation and advice you receive from a professional editor or reader, no matter how expert, is an individual's opinion and does not guarantee your manuscript's being accepted by a publishing house.

WHO ARE YOU WRITING FOR?

~

Adults who write for children go through a curious mental process. They are writing for an audience whose experience in and perspective on life is distinctly different from their own. The writer's own childhood reading experience—or life experience—may have very little relevance when it comes to writing for a contemporary young audience.

The writer must somehow develop a mind-set that ultimately leads to stories and other kinds of writing with which young readers are able to associate. At the same time the writer must convince a publisher—another adult—that a story or poem or work of non-fiction is marketable. Later on in the process, the people who choose and buy books for children are not children either, but more adults—parents, grandparents, friends, teachers, librarians, etc.

> "RESPECT THE CHARACTERS IN YOUR STORY AS MUCH AS YOU RESPECT YOURSELF."

Yet the final and most telling critic is the child. The published writer knows no thrill greater than the response of a young reader who communicates, however inarticulately, the impact a story has had. Make no mistake about it, books can have great positive influences on children. No book is going to be as important in your life as the one you read as a child.

But the writer is remote from that young reader as the writing process begins. Therefore, who is the writer writing for? Those who are beginning to write for children sometimes have preconceived ideas about what a children's book should be. But it's perhaps best to put these preconceived ideas to one side. Beginning writers have greatest success when they decide to write for themselves, write about the characters, the feelings, the themes that are most important to them. Don't assume that cuteness will appeal to children—or editors. Respect the characters in your story as much as you respect yourself. Write using every scrap of experience you possess—events in your life and the lives of those you meet, names you come across, relationships that have been important to you, settings you know well, details and insights that have stayed with you. It is within ourselves that the most powerful stories reside, and we need to trust the instincts that force those stories out onto paper.

You may not take time to consider whether you are writing to be published, and that's probably a wise approach. Your most attentive audience may simply be your own family or extended family, or friends, or the children you teach in your class. They're all deserving and important audiences.

But will your story interest a publisher? How do you know whether to edge into the professional publishing world? Your supportive friend, your writers' group, or the opinion of a professional editor may prompt you to send your work to a publisher. Their opinions may help you decide if your story can appeal to a broader audience that has no personal connection with you.

Whether you decide to move into the professional publishing world, remember that the reason you began writing in the first place was the challenge of the writing process itself, and your fascination with the challenge of capturing ideas in words, and your enjoyment in playing with language and image. Writers should never lose that initial fascination; it becomes a habit of life, a delightful obsession.

7

SENDING THE MANUSCRIPT OUT

~

If you decide to send your manuscript to a publisher, you are attempting to become a professional writer. You are acting on your ambition to make writing less a private activity and more a professional career. Of course that shift in emphasis isn't complete until you get your first publisher's contract; even then, being a professional writer isn't a secure way of making a living.

You have to know, from the outset, that the odds *against* getting your first, second, or even third manuscript published are formidable. That's why it's important to enjoy the writing process itself, rather than assuming it will be a simple matter to move easily into the role of published author. Furthermore, you should not count on your writing bringing you significant income until you have several titles published. Writers are at the bottom of the economic ladder and not a great many children's writers or illustrators are able to make a living doing nothing else but producing children's books. "Don't quit your day job!" is an important rule for aspiring writers.

Above all, don't treat publishers as sounding boards for ideas that are not fully formed. Publishers and editors are extraordinarily busy people who—while they long to stumble over that manuscript that turns their heads and makes them forget their weariness—don't appreciate ill-formed thoughts, or half-baked efforts that still need heavy rewriting; they don't welcome phone calls from winsome wannabes.

SELECTING A PUBLISHER

Several markets exist for aspiring writers of children's picture books, fiction, poetry, drama, and non-fiction. Before sending your manuscript to a specific publisher, find out whatever you can about that publisher, to make certain it is an appropriate market for your work.

While most writing for children finds its market in the publishing world, writers of drama for children are best advised to make contacts with local or regional theaters that stage plays for young people, or TV networks looking for family entertainment; note that there is a need for adaptations of existing stories as well as original work. In fact, a very small proportion of children's dramatists see their work published in book form—apart from that provided through houses that specialize in children's drama. But children's theater does have an appetite for new work, as does children's television and the film industry.

There are three major print markets for children's writing: educational, trade, and magazine.

EDUCATIONAL

The nature of educational publishing has changed in recent years—and is still in a state of flux. Some years ago, it was clear that the time had passed when each child in an elementary or junior high classroom received one textbook per subject. In fact the largest educational firms either have gone through a basic re-structuring, or have been bought out, consolidated, or closed down. Now, with education systems themselves having gone through re-structuring, more shifts and changes are occurring in educational publishing. That being said, it is still possible for beginning writers to break into print through the textbook industry, where a number of innovative projects continue to originate.

Note that educational texts are not sold in bookstores. Rather, educational publishers market directly to school boards or state or provincial or territorial departments or ministries of education.

At any one time, several educational publishers may be working on revisions of anthologies for a wide range of ages and are therefore on the lookout for short material—poems, stories, and articles. You should contact educational publishers, and ask to be put in touch with editors, to discover if and for what age level they are currently collecting material. It is best not to submit manuscripts until you know a publisher's requirements.

TRADE

Books that are sold in bookstores are called trade books. Publishers who are producing trade books for children hope they will also be able to make substantial sales to schools and libraries, though in recent years the school library market has become much less vibrant, as education systems cut back on library staff and reduce book budgets. This may not be a permanent trend, but it does affect publishing strategies. Furthermore, the powerful oncoming wave of e-readers is going to make for some major shifts in how books are marketed to young readers.

Financially, trade books make up the riskier sector of the publishing industry. The trade publisher has to make educated guesses regarding the likely success or failure of every title published, and even then success is never guaranteed. Even the most carefully conceived book project can end up a failure if the book simply doesn't sell to individual buyers. With government cutbacks and the advent of superstores, publishers may be more reluctant to take the same degree of risk in considering proposals and manuscripts from untried writers. Industry analysts point out that books that are displayed in superstores have a very short shelf-life, a matter of a few weeks at most, and unless such books are written by star authors and can sell quickly, they'll quickly disappear.

Trade publishers may specialize in certain areas of children's publishing—picture books, fiction, or non-fiction. Therefore it's wise to do research to find out which publisher is most likely to take an interest in your manuscript. You can learn a good deal by browsing through a good children's bookstore, or consulting a well-

"YOU WILL BE HAPPIEST WITH A PUBLISHER WHOSE PHILOSOPHY YOU CAN SUBSCRIBE TO WHOLEHEARTEDLY."

versed children's librarian. You should also write or call publishing houses, asking for copies of their most recent sales catalogues; or consult their websites to gather detailed information about their publishing programs, including how many books they publish and in which fields, as well as their needs. If you are an avid reader of children's books, you will already have gleaned useful information about the key players in the publishing world.

Once you become familiar with the publishers who seem most likely to be interested in your manuscript, choose ones whose style and quality most appeal to you. You will be happiest with a publisher whose philosophy you can subscribe to wholeheartedly.

Remember that trade publishers are not going to be interested in single poems or short stories—unless they are to be considered as texts for picture books.

TEEN ZINES

There are many online sites focusing on writing for, by, and about teens. The following provide you with just a few leads.

A list of teen magazines, literary and lifestyle (http://www.world-newspapers.com/youth.html). *Xenith* (http://www.xenith.net/) is a real teen literary site. *Youth Outlook* (http://www.youthoutlook.org/news/) invites submissions, and it has a non-fiction focus. *Teens Now Talk* (http://www.teensnowtalk.com/tnt/home) out of Halifax has a poetry-writing page. *Teen Voices* (http://www.teenvoices.com/) features fiction by girls for girls. *Teen Ink* (http://www.teenink.com/) features a variety of writing by teens for teens. *Faze* magazine (http://www.fazeteen.com/main.htm) is Canada's No. 1 student magazine that has a page for writing under the entertainment tab. The Madison Public Library has a solid list of magazines for kids and teens (http://www.madisonpubliclibrary.org/youth/magazines.html). *Girl Zone* (http://www.girlzone.com/expresso/) has a page for creative writing. Links to Christian magazines for teens can be found here (http://christianteens.about.com/od/christianentertainment/tp/Magazines.htm). And here are two more lists of teen magazines (http://www.dmoz.org/Kids_and_Teens/Teen_Life/Magazines_and_E-zines/) and (http://www.dmoz.org/Kids_and_Teens/Entertainment/Magazines_and_E-zines/). Finally, Scholastic has a site meant to encourage creative writing (http://blog.scholastic.com/ink_splot_26/writing-prompt/?lnkid=stacks/nav/blog/category/writing_prompts).

—Rob Morphy

MAGAZINES

There are some fine magazines that target young readers, and some of them are open to proposals for articles from unpublished writers: *OWL* and *Chickadee*, *Cricket* and *Ladybug*, *Ranger Rick* and *Highlights*, for example. You should become familiar with a magazine before you submit your project, to make sure your work suits its audience and emphasis. Look at back issues to make sure that your idea has not been used in recent months or years. Submit an outline or a query to the magazine's editor before submitting a final manuscript. Do not send the same idea or story to more than one magazine at a time.

Some fledgling magazines may not pay for published work, but offer a subscription as compensation. As a beginning writer you have to decide whether it's worthwhile working on projects that are not going to bring you income. For more information on publishers, see Section C, Part 2.

SELF-PUBLISHING

Because it usually takes time and effort and patience—and luck!—to get a manuscript published by a professional publishing house, aspiring writers are sometimes tempted by the possibility of self-publishing their work, or enlisting the expertise of companies who have come to be known as "vanity presses."

This method of getting your words into print—and your name on a book—is appealing because it seems to offer a satisfactory alternative to those sheaves of rejection slips, the tiresome business of working with an editor, the amount of time it takes for a book to be designed and produced by a professional publishing house, and the reality that your final share of the take from a commercially published book seems so small after all the energy you have expended on your project. This alternative route has become even more attractive these days because of the widespread availability of desktop publishing and the appeal of recruiting a local print shop to help you produce your book. In addition, a number of online services offer a dizzying array of self-publishing packages that make the process accessible to anyone with the money to spend.

Being in control of all aspects of writing and preparing your manuscript for publication has definite appeal. The online companies — like lulu.com, iuniverse.com, exlibris.com, and author house.com—who offer assistance for those wishing to self-publish books, make the process seem reasonable and affordable. These businesses charge for a wide range of services—everything from editing and preparing the manuscript, design, selection of format, cover selection, production, to arranging for signing events at big bookstores. For each service, the cost increases, but always the lure is the prospect of having a handsome book with your name on it in hand within a very short period of time. Such companies may also offer print-on-demand abilities—so that you don't have to cope with hundreds or thousands of copies of your book at one time. These firms also offer the option of rendering your project into ebook format.

Of course the fact that you are in control of the whole process may not prove to be a complete advantage. The production of a book is only one aspect of the publishing process (see *How a Publishing House Works*). By sidestepping the editorial, you are neglecting a crucial part of perfecting your manuscript; the editing advice you receive from these companies can be turned aside if you don't agree with it. Then there is the problem of how your self-published book is going to secure shelf-space in bookstores, gain critical reviews, and thus make its way into the hands of the buying public. How much knowhow do you have about—and how much time and money can you spend on—marketing, and promotion?

Despite the ease with which it seems you can move into this area of publishing, self-publishing can be a hazardous route to take. There are sometimes good reasons to self-publish, especially if your audience is limited and specialized—a so-called "niche" market: a group of family or friends or associates who are eager to consume the story you are telling. However, few successful children's books have been self-published, largely because there is such a lot of competition from professionally published works.

Before launching your own publishing operation, then, do careful

"THE PRODUCTION OF A BOOK IS ONLY ONE ASPECT OF THE PUBLISHING PROCESS."

research and analyze your motives for getting into the business. By taking what seems like a nice shortcut around the traditional editorial and publishing process, you may satisfy your yearning to see your words in print. But not having access to professional editorial and production advice may severely handicap your project in terms of the quality of the content.

A final caveat: some marginal publishing operations may tell you that it is now becoming customary for writers to pay for the editorial input that is a necessary part of the traditional publishing process. In fact, this claim bends the truth: the writer should not have to pay for editing the manuscript prior to publication once a contract has been signed.

8

COMMISSIONED, SOLICITED, AND
UNSOLICITED MANUSCRIPTS

~

A book project can take shape in one of several ways.
A publisher may decide to **commission** a writer to work on a particular idea for publication. This normally happens in the field of non-fiction, although it can also happen with other kinds of projects as well. Commissioned work is usually reserved for writers with a proven track record in publishing, writers whose names will help sell the book. If you are commissioned to undertake a book project, you should receive at least partial payment of advance money prior to the beginning of the writing process.

An editor may know of a writer with a manuscript in progress and **solicit** the manuscript on behalf of the publishing house. This means that the publisher is supporting the project before the writing is completed, and before it is submitted to the publishing house. Publishers will usually solicit manuscripts from writers with whom they have worked previously or writers with an established reputation.

Manuscripts which arrive unannounced in a publisher's office are called **unsolicited** manuscripts.

Most publishing houses do not rely in a major way on unsolicited manuscripts, but look for projects by already published authors whose work they know and respect.

If a typical children's publisher produces about twenty titles each year, most of them come from authors who have one or more published works to their credit. Each year, the same publisher may receive as many as two or three thousand unsolicited manuscripts.

Maybe two or three of these will end up as published books; yet editors and publishers are always on the lookout for new talent, to give their program a fresh look and to expand their stable of authors. Picture book writers Paulette Bourgeois (*Franklin in the Dark*) and Bob Munsch (*Mud Puddle*) are both examples of authors whose works arrived unannounced at publisher's offices and went on to garner international recognition and big sales.

"A FIRST BOOK CALLS FOR AN INVESTMENT—IN EDITORIAL WORK, PROMOTION, AND MARKETING—THAT WILL NOT BE REPAID FOR SOME TIME, MAYBE NOT FOR SEVERAL YEARS."

A first-time author represents a risk for a publisher. A publisher takes on a new author, hoping that the first book will be one of many the company will publish. A first book calls for an investment—in editorial work, promotion, and marketing—that will not be repaid for some time, maybe not for several years. A publisher prefers not to make an investment in a writer whose first book is his only one. A writer with a body of work to his credit, on the other hand, has a great deal of appeal to a publisher.

SUBMITTING THE MANUSCRIPT

~

Publishers respect writers who demonstrate their profession-alism by the way they submit their manuscripts.

Most publishers have websites you can consult that include submission guidelines—i.e., the form and content of manuscripts the publisher is interested in receiving. There are also a number of other resources you can consult, like *Literary Marketplace*, updated annually, which provide all sorts of information about the publishing industry. Among things you need to know before submitting your manuscript: whether companies accept email submissions or require hard copy, names of the editors or departments to which your manuscript should be addressed, kinds of projects a publisher is currently interested in looking at. Rather than sending your manuscript out into the blue without any knowledge of who will be receiving it at the other end, it's wise to do your homework first. In that way, your project stands a much better chance of being read and assessed.

Here are some general requirements you should observe:

- Manuscripts submitted to a publishing house must be clean, double-spaced, on one side of 8½" by 11" white paper. Leave a wide margin on one side of the sheet, and an inch and a half on the top and bottom of the page. Pages must be correctly numbered, with the writer's last name appearing on each sheet. Do not submit hand-written material.
- Double-check your manuscript before sending it out, to make sure all errors in spelling or typing have been corrected.
- The copyright symbol and your name, address, and phone number should appear on the title page.

- Always send a photocopy of your manuscript to a publisher; always keep your original manuscript in case copies get lost in the mail or in the publisher's office.
- If you are sending a novel, check beforehand to find out whether the publisher prefers to receive sample chapters with an outline (as most houses do), or the entire manuscript. (If a publisher wants sample chapters, you'll end up sending the complete manuscript eventually before a final decision is made.) A caution: finish writing your novel before submitting sample chapters.
- For picture books and poems, send the complete manuscript.
- For non-fiction projects, send a query letter, an outline, and some sample text.
- If you are not sure about the format for your submission— or if you aren't sure of a publisher's potential interest in your work—phone, write, or email the publisher to find out. Publishers are busy people, so don't expect to have an extensive conversation.
- Include a covering letter with your manuscript. Provide, briefly, some information about yourself, any previous publishing experience, the kind of material you are sending, and any other relevant information. A covering letter should be no longer than a page. *Do not* spend time saying how wonderful your manuscript is; that judgment is for the publisher to make.
- Enclose a self-addressed, stamped envelope (SASE) with each submission, so your manuscript can be returned to you at no cost to the publisher. Make sure the postage is sufficient to pay for the return—and, if you send the manuscript to a publisher in another country, include postage from that country, or an international postal order to cover the cost of reply. Some writers also enclose a stamped, self-addressed postcard so publishers can inform them that their manuscript has arrived safely at the publisher's office. However, some publishers may not open a package until they are ready to look at the manuscript, and this could take some months. Instead of an SASE, some writers include their email address with their submission, so publishers can

reply that way—though this means your manuscript will not be returned.

- Some publishers prefer exclusive submissions, while others accept multiple submissions. If you are submitting to more than one publisher at a time, inform each publisher that you are doing so. You do not need to tell each one the identities of other houses looking at your work.

"PUBLISHERS DO NOT LOOK FAVORABLY ON ENVELOPES THAT INCLUDE SEVERAL PROJECTS—IN FACT SOME HOUSES WILL RETURN SUCH MATERIAL UNREAD."

- You may decide to send a query before submitting a manuscript to allow a publisher to express their interest in receiving your project. This will mean a delay in a publisher actually looking at your work, but it also means that you won't be wasting postage submitting manuscripts to publishers who are not interested.

- Do not submit more than one manuscript at a time. Publishers do not look favorably on envelopes that include several projects—in fact some houses will return such material unread. It's advisable for you to make the selection of what you regard as the most appropriate project for each publisher and send that in on its own.

10

WAITING FOR THE REPLY

~

What do you do while you're waiting for an answer from the publisher? Beginning writers unwisely may put their lives—and their writing—on hold while they eagerly hang on the arrival of each day's mail. But they soon learn that the writer's life has to go on as normally as possible. The waiting period is lengthy, and there's no future in allowing your life to be governed by the anticipation of a reply.

Those who want to make writing their career—or *one* of their careers—soon learn that it's important to have several projects on the go at the same time. When one manuscript has been dropped in the mailbox, turn to developing the next one. It's healthier to occupy your mind with new work than to fret over the fate of the manuscript you've just sent away. When New Zealand children's author Margaret Mahy was first approached by a publisher, she was asked if she had any other material. She replied that she had 100 other manuscripts.

> "WHEN ONE MANUSCRIPT HAS BEEN DROPPED IN THE MAILBOX, TURN TO DEVELOPING THE NEXT ONE."

It's important that writers develop a body of work so that their skills are constantly being stretched by the challenge of new ideas and new projects, and so that their self-confidence is not solely dependent on the success of a single manuscript. Keeping up a daily writing routine can help insulate the starting writer from the blows to the ego implicit in the arrival of rejection letters. For example, one author I know currently has two manuscripts with publishers (one picture book and one non-fiction), two novels awaiting her

Handling Rejection

The dreaded R-word. It's going to happen. I was lucky; my first novel got accepted for publication. Woo Hoo! But that was only putting off the inevitable. I was also lucky in my choice of partners: my wife was an actor. Talk about rejection! Actors get rejected all the time, which made me feel a little better. But yeah, it sucks.

At some point, rejection is guaranteed. Be as angry as you want, weep, gnash your teeth, kick something (preferably not living), feel totally sorry for yourself, eat way too much ice cream, and then just get over it.

So what do you do, practically speaking? Well, if someone sends you a form letter saying: "Your story isn't right for our list," that's what they mean. They aren't saying it's bad. And they definitely aren't saying you're bad. It's not the kind of story they're looking for, period. If you're lucky enough to get feedback, read it. Does any of it sound useful? It may not be dead on, but it might contain a seed of truth. Try to pry open your mind enough to really assess what you're being told. If you keep getting the same reaction, maybe you've written a work of pure genius that no one is ready for yet. Or maybe you need to put that manuscript aside and let it rest for a bit. Whatever you do, don't get into the blame game; don't blame yourself, either.

Here's the foolproof antidote to rejection: go and write something heartbreakingly wonderful. See? That wasn't so hard, was it?

—Tim Wynne-Jones

attention, and two or three picture book ideas simmering away in the back of her mind.

It's normal to receive rejection letters from publishers to whom you first send your work. In the days of her apprenticeship as a writer, Welwyn Katz submitted a 600-page fantasy novel to a publisher who eventually rejected it. The disappointed writer burst into tears when the manuscript was returned, then sat down to work at the next project. "That's when I knew I was a writer," she says.

In fact, already-published writers can be rejected as well, even though they may have two or five or ten books in print. Kathy Stinson submitted the manuscript for *Red Is Best* to five publishers before it was accepted and eventually won an award. Subsequently she has had manuscripts rejected by several publishers, even though she has had more than twenty-five books published.

A manuscript can be rejected for all kinds of reasons. A book on a similar theme may have been recently released. The publisher who has rejected your project may be working on another book similar to yours. Perhaps the particular reader who looked at your manuscript didn't care for it; publishers' opinions are, above all, a matter of personal taste. Perhaps the publisher you've approached isn't the right one for this manuscript; some publishers will suggest other houses for you to send your manuscript to.

How long should you expect to wait for a reply from a publisher? Major children's publishers receive from two to three thousand manuscripts each year, and even smaller houses have hundreds to look at annually. It takes time to read all this material and reach decisions about it. At the very least, you should expect to wait six to eight weeks for a first reply, though some publishers take much longer, from eight months to a year.

When Publishers Miss the Boat

When former marketing guru Peter Taylor was in the book business, he was once asked to read through the stack of unsolicited manuscripts often referred to as the "slush pile." Here he discovered an absolutely brilliant novel submitted some twelve months earlier. He eagerly phoned the author to see if it was still available. The surprised author said no, but if he wanted to attend, the book launch for it was being held that very night. And that's where Peter went that night.

When you feel you have waited long enough—about three months—you are justified in contacting the publisher to find out what stage your manuscript has reached in the assembly line. You need to make this as pleasant and brief a contact as possible, because you don't want to be seen as a pest by the overworked person on the other end of the email you send, or the phone call you make.

Some publishing houses may like your manuscript on first reading and then take it through a second and third perusal by other readers, to see if the project is one they can realistically take on. This process can also take months.

If your manuscript is turned down, it will be returned to you along with a rejection letter. This may be a form letter, since publishers find it impossible to respond personally to each manuscript they receive. The fact that you've received a form letter should not be seen as a personal reflection on the quality of your work, but simply the consequence of the pressures of the publishing business. If you get a personal letter from an editor, this means your manuscript has been thoroughly considered. In this case, a publisher may indicate interest in receiving other manuscripts from you. Ironically, this should be regarded as a very positive response.

Receiving a rejection is a blow to the ego, but it is not the end of hope or career. You may decide to send your manuscript to another publisher—or you may decide to take another look at it with fresh eyes, to see if a revision could help it along.

Beginning writers may collect many rejection letters. It is important to read each rejection carefully, to understand what lies between the lines. Some rejections are not outright and total; in fact they can be encouragements. One aspiring writer I know gave up on herself as a writer after receiving a phone call from a publisher

"RECEIVING A REJECTION IS A BLOW TO THE EGO, BUT IT IS NOT THE END OF HOPE OR CAREER."

who said she could not accept the particular manuscript that had arrived at the publishing house, but said reassuringly that she would be happy to consider other book proposals. This should have been seen as positive support for the writer but it was misread as just another rejection—and the writer decided she'd had enough of getting rejected. She decided to become a singer instead.

A writer intent on learning the craft who is serious about writing will not give up in the face of one or two or more rejections, but will simply work harder. The writer who survives years of apprenticeship is probably the one who eventually finds a publisher. Persistence will out.

11

SO YOU'RE GOING TO BE PUBLISHED
. . . BUT IT'S NOT OVER YET

~

One day you go to the mail or open your computer—and you find a letter telling you a publisher wants to work with you to produce a book. Hallelujah! You're going to be published!

But wait just a minute: all the work isn't done yet.

Acceptance can mean a number of things. The publisher may want you to do minor or major surgery on the text before offering you a contract. Or you may be offered a contract immediately, because the publisher doesn't think there is much work left to do on your manuscript. (One picture book writer had to do thirteen rewrites of his first accepted story *after* it was contracted by the publisher.) Best of all, you may be offered a contract that calls for a payment to you in advance of publication.

The point is: the writing process enters another stage when a publisher accepts your manuscript. Acceptance means that you will begin to work with an editor. Up to now, you have been the sole creator of your manuscript. Now you are entering into a business relationship with a company that wishes to publish your work. And the editor is your main partner in this enterprise. The editor's role is to work with you to produce the best book possible from your manuscript. The editor is able to stand back and see where polishing and rewriting can improve what you've written. As the writer, you have been so close to the manuscript that it's difficult to look at your work objectively. The editor is a friendly adviser who can pick out the remaining flaws and suggest ways to eliminate them. An editor,

On Getting that First "Yes"

The working title of what became *Franklin in the Dark* was *The Turtle They Called Chicken*, because in the manuscript I sent so eagerly to publishers in the US and Canada in 1984, Franklin was taunted by his friends because he was "too chicken" to go inside his small dark shell. Perhaps I went too far when I wrote:

His friends yelled: "You yellow-bellied, chicken-livered, spineless excuse for a turtle." Some of them called him claustrophobic. It was terrible. Franklin didn't even know what that meant.

Yes, I really did write those words and sent them out to the biggest publishers across Canada and the US. Perhaps the abusive language was the reason that letter after letter, six in all, came back informing me that although they had given my story "careful consideration" they could not offer to publish it.

I was terribly discouraged and convinced that I would never write another picture book, when I chanced upon a course offering to teach me how to write children's books taught by Peter Carver. I was learning a lot and feeling hopeful when just before the third class and on the day that Kids Can publisher Valerie Hussey was scheduled to speak to the class, I received the letter that would change my life as a writer. I was, to use a cliché, over the moon. Valerie herself wrote the letter, telling me that the story needed to be honed and expanded. She also wrote, "I wouldn't overstate the ridicule that is hurled at Franklin, either. The children-reader will feel his humiliation; you don't want to make the reader uncomfortable." Excellent advice. I still get rejection letters but I prefer the ones that say, "We are in fact quite interested." Those little words from a publisher gave me an entire new direction in my life.

—Paulette Bourgeois

however, is not a writer and will expect you to do the revisions and rewriting yourself.

The editor may be on the staff of the publishing house, but is just as likely to be a freelancer hired by the publisher specifically for your project. In either case, the editor is employed by the publisher, not by you, and has to bring together the interests of the publisher and the writer and the reader.

The editor will get to know your manuscript as well as you do.

The relationship between writer and editor is a delicate and fascinating one. Some writers object to changing a word of their manuscript: this is not usually the way to produce the best possible book, or to get your book published at all, for that matter. On the other hand, beginning writers in particular tend to cave in to all suggestions made by an editor. Neither extreme is desirable. You want to retain the essential integrity of your manuscript and yet listen to intelligent and sensitive comments and suggestions from your editor. Editors and publishers respect writers who can defend their work, but who are prepared to listen to suggestions for change.

"SOME WRITERS OBJECT TO CHANGING A WORD OF THEIR MANUSCRIPT: THIS IS NOT USUALLY THE WAY TO PRODUCE THE BEST POSSIBLE BOOK, OR TO GET YOUR BOOK PUBLISHED AT ALL, FOR THAT MATTER. ON THE OTHER HAND, BEGINNING WRITERS IN PARTICULAR TEND TO CAVE IN TO ALL SUGGESTIONS MADE BY AN EDITOR. NEITHER EXTREME IS DESIRABLE."

If you have had a picture book text accepted by a publisher, of course, another level of engagement comes into play—the choice of an illustrator for your project. Though you will have a strong interest in that choice, it's a decision that is made by the publisher.

B

FOR THE ILLUSTRATOR

...

1

WORKING AS AN ILLUSTRATOR

~

The publishing world offers a variety of opportunities to illustrators, and nowhere are the opportunities more exciting than in the realm of children's books. Picture books in particular give illustrators lots of room to express themselves and allow the kind of freedom and control over their work that simply can't be found in most sectors of the commercial art world. Illustrating non-fiction books for children also presents exciting challenges, though the work is obviously more narrowly focused on a given subject not of the illustrator's choosing.

But working on a picture book or a heavily illustrated non-fiction title is specialized, demanding, and time-consuming work. Very few illustrators can afford to do books all the time, and so, almost by definition, illustrators are people who work for a range of clients—advertising and commercial art firms, newspapers, magazines, educational, and trade publishers.

Working as an illustrator means you must know the language, the terminology of the commercial art and publishing world. The education of an illustrator comes from a combination of training and experience, both of which are necessary before you can hope to work on a picture book.

Book publishers are constantly on the lookout for new illustrating talent. As the children's book industry has grown and matured, so has the demand for illustrators possessed of vision and skill. Work is available, not just in picture books and non-fiction, but also in children's magazines, website design, and in the creation of cover illustrations for novels.

2

ILLUSTRATING PICTURE BOOKS

~

In some ways, now is a time of great opportunity for would-be illustrators of picture books. Digital technology and sophisticated printing methods can result in magnificent books vibrant with color and designed to draw the attention of young readers. In some ways, though, this is also a time when picture book production has become so costly that the market is shrinking and the chances for getting work as a picture book illustrator are becoming rarer.

For the past thirty years and more, the quality and diversity of picture books produced round the world have been extraordinary. Not only have art schools turned out well-trained illustrators who have been schooled in the language of production, but a significant number of gallery artists have been drawn into the enticing possibilities of illustration of high-end picture books. Too, the audience for picture books extends from the very young to readers who have begun to read chapter books, but still retain a taste for the rich and "THE ILLUSTRATOR'S JOB IS TO CREATE POWERFUL IMAGES TO STIMULATE YOUNG IMAGINATIONS." lively art to be found in picture books with themes that are more demanding and layered. For many readers, the art found in the pages of a picture book is their introduction to visual art, its range and texture and subject matter. To become immersed in those pages is one of the most powerful experiences a young reader can have.

With the difficulties of increased costs, though, publishers have learned to be far more discriminating in choosing picture book projects on which to spend their energy and money. So aspiring illustrators need to be far more skilled and tenacious if they wish to enter this field.

Illustrations for picture books range from highly detailed pencil and line drawings through watercolor and gouache to full-blown oil paintings to computerized digital art. The illustrator's job is to create powerful images to stimulate young imaginations. Children are introduced to visual art through the illustrations in the picture books they read; thus the role of the illustrator is a critical one in the cultural development of the child.

In producing a picture book, the writer and illustrator are equal partners. While the story usually begins with the writer's words, the pictures carry their own narrative thread and can often contain details not found in the text. This is the challenge and the opportunity for the picture book illustrator.

Incidentally, while many illustrators are tempted by the idea of writing their own text as well as creating the artwork, the two skills may not be present in the same person. Some well-known illustrators—Chris van Allsburg, Barbara Cooney, Ed Young, Marie-Louise Gay, Barbara Reid among them—both write and illustrate. But many illustrators, even those who write, also enjoy the team approach to producing a picture book in which writer, illustrator, and designer each have their separate roles to play, their own strengths to draw on.

While the market for picture book illustrators has increased, the competition is much stiffer today than it was twenty years ago.

"IN PRODUCING A PICTURE BOOK, THE WRITER AND ILLUSTRATOR ARE EQUAL PARTNERS."

Publishers want to see portfolios that demonstrate an illustrator's ability to sustain a character or characters through a story, a distinct illustrating style, and a mastery of different media. If as an illustrator you have already had work published, this will help convince an art director or publisher of your professional knowledge of production techniques and the printing process. Most illustrators today create their own websites to display their art to potential clients—which means that portfolios are readily available without having to involve expensive and risky mailings or courier deliveries.

3

ILLUSTRATING NON-FICTION

~

As the children's book industry has matured, certain publishers have become renowned internationally for the quality and diversity of their non-fiction titles. The impact of the British firm of Dorling Kindersley on the look and range of information book publishing has been immense in the past two decades. DK, as it's known familiarly, publishes for both children and adults, and in the children's field everything from infant boardbooks to encyclopedias for teenagers. DK publishes under its own imprint, but also prepares series that appear under various other publishers' names; you find DK's name in the small print on the copyright pages of these books. For years, the influence of this one company has extended across national boundaries and languages, and the approach taken in its books has affected many other publishers.

"A VERSATILE ILLUSTRATOR IS WELL-SERVED TODAY BY GAINING TRAINING AND KNOWLEDGE IN THE COMPUTER DESIGN FIELD—AS WELL AS A PRACTICAL WORKING KNOWLEDGE IN THE USE OF TYPE-FACES."

Illustration is a significant component of successful non-fiction for young readers. There is no question that the influence of the media has affected the presentation of information to young people. In a typical DK book, each spread can consist of up to ten or twelve nuggets of information in text, each accompanied by a visual component, and each spread can be read by itself without reference to the rest of the pages in the book; powerful, colorful, and easily consumed information in a media age.

Some illustrators have become specialists in producing stunning and informative visual art for information and craft books. The demand for imaginative rendering of a subject is just as vital as the need to convey information clearly and unmistakably. Research skills come to the fore when you are responsible for producing art for a book on space, or baseball, or schoolyard games.

TRAINING AND BACKGROUND

~

How do you become a children's book illustrator?

The first step is to find art courses that provide thorough training in commercial art and design. Being a Sunday painter or an occasional dabbler doesn't provide the kind of intensive training you're going to need. Most colleges of art have departments of commercial art, and while courses in children's illustration may not be offered separately, the information and experience available in this field is extremely useful.

If you would like to work as a children's book illustrator, you also need to do research, in libraries and bookstores, to acquaint yourself with the work now being done in this field. You may be surprised to find out just how accomplished children's book illustration has become. You'll notice the range of artwork, from the simpler cartoon style that makes such a direct appeal to children, through to the elegant and more painterly illustrations found in what some might call coffee-table picture books. As you look for a publisher who might want to work with you, think about where you might find the most congenial home for your personality and your artwork.

Work experience is the next step along the road. Most individuals who illustrate children's books began working in some sector of the commercial art world. This kind of experience allows you to learn the terminology of commercial illustration and production, which is essential if you want to break into the picture book field. Working with experienced art directors and designers teaches you the distinction between black and white line work, two-color, three-color, and four-color illustration.

Today, with the flood of digital production, a whole new area of opportunity has opened up with the advent of sophisticated computerized design and illustration techniques. Many trade picture books, some projects for educational publishers, as well as non-fiction trade books, make use of computer design packages. A versatile illustrator is well-served today by gaining training and knowledge in the computer design field—as well as a practical working knowledge in the use of type-faces.

"WORKING WITH EXPERIENCED ART DIRECTORS AND DESIGNERS TEACHES YOU THE DISTINCTION BETWEEN BLACK AND WHITE LINE WORK, TWO-COLOR, THREE-COLOR, AND FOUR-COLOR ILLUSTRATION."

5

STARTING OUT

~

What are the chances of breaking into the book publishing world? As already noted, the picture book market has been shrinking over the past ten years, but there are still many books for children in the non-fiction realm that make use of skilled and imaginative artists. As well, a number of publishers use illustration, rather than stock or original photography, for book covers for their fiction titles—though the scene is changing yearly.

So, pounding the pavement are hundreds of illustrators looking for opportunities in the publishing world—though now many of those opportunities are to be found in the new media rather than traditional publishing.

The starting point for many successful picture book illustrators has been the educational publishing industry. Educational publishers are constantly revising existing textbooks and creating new educational programs for primary and secondary schools. These programs cover a wide range of subject areas—mathematics, science, social studies, language arts, French, and others—and therefore offer plenty of scope for the creative illustrator. Educational publishing can be a good source of income for illustrators and provides useful training as well, though turn-around times these days make the work more high-pressure. Illustrators who have made their mark in the trade (picture books, non-fiction, book covers) often continue to work in this field, since there are usually more opportunities. It is only after you've done several successful picture books that continue to sell well, that you may be able to afford to specialize as a picture book illustrator. Even then, however, most professional illustrators look for opportunities outside the traditional book world. These days, the growth area for illustrators and graphic designers is in the field of web design and illustration for online markets.

"IT IS ONLY AFTER YOU'VE DONE SEVERAL SUCCESSFUL PICTURE BOOKS THAT CONTINUE TO SELL WELL, THAT YOU MAY BE ABLE TO AFFORD TO SPECIALIZE AS A PICTURE BOOK ILLUSTRATOR."

6

MAKING THE APPROACH: PLANNING YOUR PORTFOLIO

~

Showing portfolios is how illustrators demonstrate their abilities to a publishing house. Therefore it is crucial to prepare a portfolio carefully, in order to leave the best impression possible and thereby attract work in future. Even if there is no work available right away, a publisher will keep track of a new illustrator whose portfolio makes a strong impression and may well contact you when a new project arrives in the publishing house. Note that, in the new media age, portfolios are more frequently seen online than sent by post or courier to prospective clients.

Publishers want to see a wide range of your work, published and unpublished. They want to know that you understand the language of production art. They want to know whether you can do realistic portrayals of animals and people (particularly children), whether you are a good cartoonist, whether you have a good sense of color and design, whether your art is clean and precise, whether you are able to work in different media. They also want to see a definite personality in your work, a style which would be recognizable in a picture book. They will want to see tear sheets, or the electronic equivalent, from your published work. All these elements should be present in your portfolio. If you have not yet worked on a book professionally, take some time to prepare a "dummy" book

"PUBLISHERS WANT TO SEE A WIDE RANGE OF YOUR WORK, PUBLISHED AND UNPUBLISHED."

(a digital version is most cost effective) that will demonstrate your ability to take characters through a story and to work with type; though this may represent some cost in time and money, it can serve as a showcase of your skills. Before contacting a publisher it's wise to do some research so you know something about the kind of projects a particular house is producing, and have a sense of how your style could fit in with the tone and personality of the publisher's books. Consult their websites, get to know something about them—that will impress

"THEY WANT TO KNOW THAT YOU UNDERSTAND THE LANGUAGE OF PRODUCTION ART. THEY WANT TO KNOW WHETHER YOU CAN DO REALISTIC PORTRAYALS OF ANIMALS AND PEOPLE (PARTICULARLY CHILDREN), WHETHER YOU ARE A GOOD CARTOONIST, WHETHER YOU HAVE A GOOD SENSE OF COLOR AND DESIGN, WHETHER YOUR ART IS CLEAN AND PRECISE, WHETHER YOU ARE ABLE TO WORK IN DIFFERENT MEDIA."

How to Approach a Publisher

For wannabe book illustrators a web presence is essential—it's the first place to go. If you can't afford a website (or don't have enough material yet), signing up for one of the collective websites would be the next choice. Many book illustrators are on sites like childrensillustrators.com—there are several of these. Having your own website is best though, because you can control it and it should become the first place people go for current and accurate information. If someone finds you on a collective, it looks professional if they can then link to your own site. A blog section can keep it fresh, but don't blog on blog sites—just on your own site. That way people are going to you, you aren't promoting someone else's ads. All web exposure should bring people to your site.

The next important thing is mailing hard copy—postcards or a sample sheet. It is becoming cheaper and easier all the time to produce good quality samples. Art directors still like to pin things up on their walls, and direct mail is more powerful than just getting email. Emails may get lost or ignored by busy art directors (ADs). But the postcard will send them to a site if it catches their eye.

It is still very useful to meet ADs with an actual portfolio when possible. Maybe the portfolio is on a laptop, or tablet, but face to face is still a good way to make an impression. Personality is a factor for both sides if working together. ADs are still easier to meet than editors. That being said, it's not all that necessary—I did an ad job last year without meeting or even speaking on the phone with the creative team. Young people are very comfortable with digital relationships, and quite articulate. And now, a lot of illustration is digital anyway, and the artist can live anywhere.

As to what goes into a portfolio—that hasn't changed much. Good, original, child-centered stuff that suits the publisher. Same old "do your research" applies. Eight excellent samples trump twenty-five mediocre ones. Persistence pays off; keep mailing and calling. If they haven't heard from you in six months, they may assume you have moved on to shoe sales or waiting tables. Promote, network, stay fresh and update your material.

—Barbara Reid

....

the art director (AD) or editor when you refer to books they have already published.

If you do manage to sit down with an AD, editor, or publisher to show your work, it's a good idea to keep a few things in mind: don't be intimidated, but don't behave as if hiring you will be the answer to all the publisher's problems. Be ready to talk about related experience and people you've worked for, but don't complain about other designers or companies you've been associated with. There's also no need to leave original artwork with a publisher.

7

GETTING HIRED

~

By showing your portfolio and keeping in touch with publishing houses, you make yourself known and lay the groundwork for being hired to illustrate a picture book or non-fiction title. Publishers also consult commercial art reference material such as *Creative Source* to look for new talent.

When you are hired for a job, you will work in collaboration with several individuals who are also involved in the project. The editor of the manuscript, the publisher's art director, the book designer, and maybe even the writer will all be part of the team producing the book. Smaller publishers do not employ art directors on their staffs, and you will likely work with the book designer. In some cases, it's the illustrator who is asked to create the book design (if that person has enough basic knowledge of the field). Design involves choosing type, planning page layouts, and sharing responsibility for deciding on the size and shape of the finished book.

A children's picture book is characteristically twenty-four or thirty-two pages long. This means that the illustrator is called on to execute art for the cover in addition to from ten to seventeen "spreads" (including title page and endpapers) in the book, which could translate to twenty or more individual illustrations, depending on the design of each spread. (For example, a spread may call for one large illustration spread over two pages, or one illustration for each page, or several smaller "spot" illustrations.)

The first stage of work on the book is preparing thumbnails— or storyboards—that show in very rough sketch form what each spread will contain, and demonstrate the flow of the story visually.

As the illustrator gains confidence in and understanding of the content of the book, thumbnails are worked up into black and white roughs. From these may come color roughs, or the illustrator may move directly into final art. As work progresses, the illustrator may work closely with the author of the text, or the two may never meet or consult. Some publishers prefer that author and illustrator do not meet or communicate so that the two narrative lines are kept quite distinct, while others enjoy seeing what can emerge from a closer partnership. One prolific picture book author has nothing at all to do with his books once he submits the manuscript; the first time he sees the art is when he receives his copies of the finished book. On the other hand, another recent picture book was set in the author's childhood neighborhood, and the author provided the illustrator with photos and memorabilia to aid in her accurate representation of the story's setting. Whichever the case, an illustrator may discover elements of the text that need change, to accommodate the artwork; at the same time, an author who is able to participate in this stage of creating the book may want to have some of the illustration details altered to complement the text more effectively.

> "WORK ON A PICTURE BOOK CAN TAKE AS LITTLE AS TWO OR THREE MONTHS OR AS LONG AS A YEAR OR EVEN TWO, DEPENDING ON THE STYLE OF ARTWORK CALLED FOR ON A PARTICULAR PROJECT— AND DEPENDING ON THE WAY THE ARTIST WORKS."

Work on a picture book can take as little as two or three months or as long as a year or even two, depending on the style of artwork called for on a particular project—and depending on the way the artist works. A non-fiction project can certainly occupy at least a year of an illustrator's life and work-time. As an illustrator becomes more experienced, more time may be spent on creating the final illustrations so that every nuance can be considered and included. At the same time, a lot of the artist's time is spent in the initial planning and research stage—often more time than is needed for the final art. Having said all this, it's unfortunately true that sometimes the production of a picture book may be a rush job, governed by tight deadlines that force an illustrator to complete final art in as little as six weeks.

An illustrator must always be prepared for her work to be

critiqued and revisions called for as a project develops. The "vision" for a book is ultimately the publisher's, and being professional as an illustrator means submitting to the judgment of the company that has hired you. If worst comes to worst, a publisher may decide to institute a "kill fee" to remove you from a project if it's felt the creative relationship is no longer working, or if the artwork is not of the quality or style the book calls for.

"AN ILLUSTRATOR MUST ALWAYS BE PREPARED FOR HER WORK TO BE CRITIQUED AND REVISIONS CALLED FOR AS A PROJECT DEVELOPS."

THE ILLUSTRATOR AS FREELANCER

~

Most illustrators are freelancers. That is, they work for themselves, contracting out their services to their clients, including publishers, for specific jobs. You may find that one publisher wants to give you enough work to keep you busy all the time. You remain a freelancer, but in fact you are occupied in working for a single client. This situation is rare. More typically, illustrators find they are working for more than one publisher, and have several projects on the go or waiting for start-up. A single publisher will not usually be able to assign an illustrator more than one picture book or non-fiction project a year. You will need to keep on the lookout for a variety of jobs—some in book publishing, some in newspapers and magazines, some in the commercial advertising world, some in online media—in order to make a living as an illustrator.

Juggling your responsibilities to a number of different clients is part of the illustrator's precarious but stimulating life. You may find yourself doing picture books with one publisher, working on a non-fiction title for another, and accepting work for educational publishers at the same time. Creating posters, editorial cartoons, commercial art for newspapers and magazines, and web design for Internet clients can help supplement your income.

Some illustrators like to use their spare time for the creation of fine art for gallery showings. In recent years others have discovered that there is a developing market in the sale of original art for illustrations to the private market. In other words, sometimes you can find an additional source of income by selling the pieces of art you have created for a book.

The more experience you gain in a variety of fields, the more you bring to your work as a children's book illustrator.

C

FOR WRITERS AND ILLUSTRATORS

...

1

HOW A PUBLISHING HOUSE WORKS

~

As the book you work on, as either author or illustrator, goes through the production process, you will learn more and more about the way a publishing house operates. To the newcomer, the publisher's office may seem like a disorganized jungle, but in fact a number of vital jobs are being done, all of which are necessary to getting your book edited and produced, sent out to the bookstores, and sold. Each publishing company has its own character and idiosyncrasies, but all have certain functions in common. A large publishing house may break down its work into any number of specialized areas. In a small company, one person performs several of the functions described below.

- The publisher is the person responsible for the overall running of the company, hiring and firing staff, negotiating contracts, making final decisions about the publishing program, and making sure that all schedules and budgets are kept to. In Canada, where publishing houses are rarely financially comfortable, the publisher must also keep track of government grant programs that help keep the company in business.
- The editor's job is to guide the writer through the development of his book. The editor also is in charge of acquiring new manuscripts and making recommendations on upcoming projects; a company's children's editor will be in charge of that publisher's children's publishing program, which could consist of anywhere from a handful to dozens of books a

season. In addition, the editor sees each book through the production process, making sure that each member of the team is performing well and on schedule. Sometimes the "in-house" editor (the publisher's employee) will contract a freelance editor to work on a specific book, delegating responsibility for that project to the freelancer. In a large publishing house, the jobs of acquiring new manuscripts, supervising projects, designing the publishing program, and seeing each book through the production stage may be divided amongst several individuals. In a small publishing house, one person performs all these functions.

- The art director, who may be on the publishing house staff or hired on a freelance basis, is responsible for the overall look of the books published by the company, and also works with the illustrator of each title to make sure that the art blends with or complements the text.

- The designer is assigned to work on a specific book. There is a designer responsible for every book published, even for novels in which the designer's job focuses on preparing a cover and making technical decisions about the type and layout of the pages. In all but the largest publishing houses, the designer is usually a freelancer. In smaller houses, the art director and designer can be the same person. In the computer age, designers tend to be responsible for generating type for the body of the text, as well as for titles. Computer technology has made obsolete the work that used to be done by the typesetter and the paste-up specialist; now the work is all done on-screen by the designer.

- The production department coordinates the overall scheduling of a manuscript's progress through the stages required to produce a finished book. The production manager works with the editor and designer to make sure that the production timetable is kept, and is responsible for making arrangements for color proofs and print, functions which are usually done on contract by outside firms.

- Promotions and publicity may be handled by a whole department or a single individual, depending on the size of the publishing house. It is the responsibility of this department to generate as much publicity as possible for each new title on the publisher's list—including personal appearances by the author, review copies sent to critics, advertisements in newspapers and magazines, and other kinds of promotional events.

- Marketing and sales managers arrange for the production of sales catalogues, the organization of sales conferences for the representatives who sell the books, and the supervision of the company's sales force. In fact, the marketing department is a vital part of any publishing company, since a decision whether to go ahead with a project will often depend on the degree to which there appears to be a market for the prospective book. More and more, particularly in larger publishing houses, it is the marketing department that has the definitive role in shaping a publishing program.

- The accounting department's job is to keep the publishing house solvent—publishing is always a risky business—and to make sure that bills are paid to printers and other suppliers. Accounting is also responsible for sending you your regular royalty checks.

Depending on the size of the company, there may be additional editorial assistants, production staff, sales people, and administrators in charge of special series or lines of titles. In North America, active publishing houses range in size from one or two people to 150 or 200.

Because publishing is a volatile business, considerable turnover occurs in the staff of any firm—and these days changes in ownership can seriously affect a publishing program. Therefore it is worthwhile keeping in touch with publishers you are working with—or would like to work with—to keep yourself informed about the identity of the key personnel and the company's publishing list.

2

HOW TO FIND A PUBLISHER

~

Part of your job as an aspiring writer or illustrator is to acquaint yourself with the publisher or publishers to whom you plan to send your manuscript or artwork.

Publishing children's books requires specialized knowledge, not just in assessing of manuscripts being looked at, but also in understanding the market and the way in which books for children sell. Some publishers have taken a great deal of trouble to educate themselves about what attracts children to books, while others depend on vague memories of children's books from another time to guide them. Those who are the most successful marketers of children's books know that the true best-seller is one that continues to sell for five or ten years—or even decades; one of the real bonuses for those creating quality children's books is that the best books are always finding a new audience. For the most successful publishers, a good portion of that audience has been found in the school classroom and library. Yet with the strain on educational budgets, the school market is not such a significant part of that sales picture.

So, how to find a publisher for your manuscript?

It doesn't take long to locate lists of publishers who are open to receiving unsolicited material. Whether it's the Canadian Children's Book Center (CCBC) or the Society of Children's Book Writers and Illustrators (SCBWI), such lists are readily acquired. There are also

> "ONE OF THE REAL BONUSES FOR THOSE CREATING QUALITY CHILDREN'S BOOKS IS THAT THE BEST BOOKS ARE ALWAYS FINDING A NEW AUDIENCE."

numerous books and resources online that can provide signposts for the writers' market in general and the children's market in particular. In a way there's almost too much information available. It's like being given the roadmap for a large country you've never visited and then trying to find the place where you're likely to feel most at home.

By now, you've probably gathered that it's your research as a reader of children's books that is going to help orient you best. Through identifying the books you find most appealing—and their publishers—you can begin to accustom yourself in this new world you know so little about. Browse through websites to find out more about those publishers whose books you are most drawn to. It may be that you're taken with large houses that have names that resonate in the market—legendary firms that have published famous authors and illustrators whose company you yearn to enjoy. But it may

"BUT IT MAY BE SENSIBLE TO LOOK FOR SMALLER PRESSES AND REGIONAL HOUSES WHICH COULD BE MORE RECEPTIVE TO SOMEONE TRYING TO GET HIS FOOT IN THE DOOR."

be sensible to look for smaller presses and regional houses which could be more receptive to someone trying to get his foot in the door. Big publishing companies might offer handsome advances, but they are deluged with so many submissions that they have in many cases insisted that they will only deal with agents. Smaller presses often provide that crucial first opportunity, the training ground for fresh talent, that a solid publishing industry depends on.

The publishing world is in a volatile state in the early 21st century, and therefore the aspiring writer needs to keep up regularly with the most recent configurations, retirements, and new appearances. It's your job to become professionally knowledgeable about who is where, which office is likely to be the most receptive to the particular project you want to submit.

While some houses implode from time to time or are absorbed into larger conglomerates, it's encouraging to find that new small houses have opened and are doing quality work.

3

COPYRIGHT

~

How do you protect your work from those who might want to present it as their own—or sell it, distribute it, or download it without your consent? The protection of intellectual property is a concern for all authors and illustrators. Copyright is a way of protecting what you have created, making sure you get credit for it, and are paid for its use. When something you have created is published, it is done with the understanding that you have agreed to its publication.

Copyright is a national and international system of laws and conventions that most countries in the world have agreed to uphold. This system attempts to protect the creators of original work.

However, copyright does not protect ideas. Ideas are free to anyone who cares to use them. When you talk to people about an idea for a story or a play or a poem or a painting, there is no guarantee against another person taking your idea and using it. Certain ideas tend to emerge at certain times and may turn up in various places. For example, some years ago many children's publishers began working on books about the environment. Because concern about the environment has been so pervasive in our society, it was inevitable that young readers would be interested in books on this topic. The result has been a flood of books on various environmental themes, some of them duplicating each other. The idea was out there, and writers and publishers acted on their instincts to produce useful and interesting books.

If you are entering the publishing field for the first time you may worry that your work will be stolen by someone else, and that you will not get credit for your work. However, there are various ways in which you can guard your copyright.

- On the title page of your work, place the copyright symbol © beside your name, with the date.
- You can establish copyright by mailing a copy of your work to yourself by registered mail. When you receive the envelope, do *not* open it but put it in a safe place. This will prove that on the date showing on the registering stamp, you owned this property.
- In Canada, if your work includes tables, charts, and other technical information, you may want to register copyright with The Copyright Office, Canadian Intellectual Properties Agency, 50 Victoria Street, Hull Quebec K1A 0C9; (900) 565-2476 ($3 flat call); http://strategis.ic.gc.ca/sc_mrksv/cipo/cp/cp_main-e.html
- Write to The Copyright Office for the appropriate forms. Complete the forms and return them with a small fee; this will register your copyright—you do not have to send the original work. For more information about this procedure, contact The Copyright Office.
- In the US, you need to register with the US Copyright Office (Library of Congress), 101 Independence Avenue, S.E. Washington, D.C. 20559-6000, (202) 707-3000, http://www.copyright.gov/eco, before you are able to make a claim in a US court. Registration may also entitle you to statutory damages in a US court case. Obtain Form TX or Short Form TX (choose which form to use) from the Library of Congress. Fill out the application and post it along with a copy of your work and the registration fee. If your submission is in order, you should receive a certificate of registration in about four to five months.
- A useful tip: by law all literary works are copyrighted the moment they are created. Nothing needs to be filed, though copyright-filing companies would like you to believe otherwise. Registering a copyright will serve only to support your claim should anyone try to steal your work. Most reputable publishers and agents see an author's copyrighting

of his or her manuscript to be a mark of amateurism. Professional writers do not copyright manuscripts.

Many writers have become concerned about the implications of photocopying books and periodicals. The result has been the setting up of Access Copyright, which seeks to protect original works from unlimited photocopying. To learn more about this new level of copyright, write Access Copyright, Suite 1900, One Yonge Street, Toronto, Ontario M5E 1E6 (416) 868-1620; info@accesscopyright. ca. In the United States go to the Copyright Clearance Center, 222 Rosewood Drive, Danvers, MA 01923, USA; 978-750-8400; info@ copyright.com; http://www.copyright.com.

With the advent of the Internet and digital technology, a whole new realm of copyright concerns has emerged. While existing copyright law could be said to apply to new modes of information dispersal, the very nature of the electronic media makes it more difficult to enforce copyright provisions now appearing in the contracts writers and illustrators sign with their publishers. For example, the very existence of electronic scanners makes it possible for whole books to be transmitted on the Internet, and there is very little one can do to monitor the downloading of such material. Even though

"WITH THE ADVENT OF THE INTERNET AND DIGITAL TECHNOLOGY A WHOLE NEW REALM OF COPYRIGHT CONCERNS HAS EMERGED."

the specter of wide-open illegal access to intellectual property is daunting, it is important that your contract with a publisher does take into account the "moral rights" that you hold. Make certain there are clauses that define your arrangements with the publisher regarding all digital usage including ebooks.

Copyright laws in Canada and the US are changing in the face of new book transmittal technologies and changes of government, while the development of electronic publishing has raised a complex network of new concerns about the rights of creators of texts and pictures. The future is murky when it comes to anticipating just what these implications might be.

A final note about copyright: in the context of your novel or work of non-fiction you may wish to quote from works by other authors. In that event, you need to ascertain your responsibilities regarding such use. Just as your words and images are your intellectual property, so is that of other authors and illustrators theirs. Employing other people's words for use in your own project involves seeking permission, and possibly paying a fee for that use.

4

HOW DO YOU GET PAID?

~

Writers and illustrators are generally paid for their work in one of two ways: fee or royalty. If a book is to be published professionally by a reputable firm, it is usually preferable for writer or illustrator to be paid on a royalty basis, although this isn't an absolute rule.

Some publishers like to retain copyright for the text in books they produce, and therefore pay the writer a fee. What this means is that a writer is guaranteed a fixed payment for the work done, the amount of which is not dependent on the number of books sold. In this way, if the book doesn't sell well, the writer still gets the complete fee. But a fee arrangement can work against the writer's interests if a book sells well, because she isn't making anything on succeeding print runs. Decades ago, Leslie McFarlane was the author of more than twenty of the famous *Hardy Boys* mysteries—published under the pseudonym Franklin W. Dixon—and his arrangement with Edward Stratemeyer, the publisher who hired him, gave him a flat fee of sometimes less than $100 a book, no matter how many copies sold.

> "THE TOTAL ROYALTY CAN RANGE CONSIDERABLY, BUT PUBLISHERS GENERALLY PAY FROM EIGHT (FOR SOFT COVER) TO TEN PERCENT (HARD COVER)."

For this reason, most writers prefer a royalty arrangement. This calls for the writer to receive a percentage of the selling price (usually referred to as list price) of each book sold. The total royalty can range considerably, but publishers generally pay from eight (for soft cover) to ten percent (hard cover). If a book sells for five dollars and the agreed-upon royalty is ten percent, the writer receives 50 cents for each book sold. Lower royalty percentages apply to book-club and educational sales and other special markets. And if your book is being produced by a book packager (a company that produces a book and sells the entire print run to another publisher) you may find your share of the take reduced to an even lower percentage, or expressed as a share of the profits. Advice from a lawyer or someone who knows about contracts is essential when you're confronted with such variations.

Most authors receive an advance against royalties payable before the book is published. An advance may be paid all at once or in staged instalments—the first on signing the contract, a second when the manuscript is finalized, and a final payment when the book is published. Advances can range from a few hundred dollars to several thousand dollars, and of course the amount is deducted from future royalties. A writer receiving an advance not only has the pleasure

> "ADVANCES CAN RANGE FROM A FEW HUNDRED DOLLARS TO SEVERAL THOUSAND DOLLARS, AND OF COURSE THE AMOUNT IS DEDUCTED FROM FUTURE ROYALTIES."

of seeing some money in the bank prior to publication, but also can have some confidence that the publisher intends to go about promoting and marketing the book aggressively, so that the advance won't represent a net loss to the publisher.

For a picture book project, the royalty arrangement usually calls for a split in royalties between writer and illustrator. It was once the practice for publishers to contract for an uneven split—based on the perceived relative drawing power of writer and illustrator—but now usually the split is even.

A picture book illustrator may be paid an advance, some or all of it payable before work begins on the project. This advance may be against royalties, or it may be a fee which is quite separate from royalties, or it may be a combination of the two.

For illustrators who work on non-fiction titles, payment has until recently been on a fee basis, often in staged payments, rather than royalties. The reasoning by publishers is that illustrations in non-fiction are more incidental to the book's success than they are in picture books; therefore the writer receives the entire royalty and the illustrator gets a fee. But currently some of the leading publishers of non-fiction are offering their illustrators a share of royalties, in recognition of the major contribution an illustrator makes to a successful book.

An illustrator who is offered a fee should find out exactly how much work is involved in the book project before agreeing to a price, to make sure that the fee is adequate. In calculating the amount of work involved in a project, the illustrator will want to pin down how much research is required to produce the finished illustrations, and just how much detail is needed in the final art. Publishers may ask for spot rather than half-page or full-page illustrations, but smaller pictures may require just as much detailed work as larger ones.

For both authors and illustrators, it is a good idea to compare notes with others in the field to make sure that the amount and method of payment offered by a publisher is comparable with similar arrangements made in the industry. Illustrators trying to break into the field will have to accept the fact that they are not going to receive the level of payment accorded more experienced artists. An untried illustrator could receive an advance as low as $500 for a project for which an established artist would get $5,000, $10,000— or more. Similarly, a first-time author is not going to receive the level of advance that is paid to an established author.

It is only realistic to be prepared for the fact that not all the provisions you would wish for, as a first-time author or illustrator, will be written into your contract. Through negotiating the terms of your first published book, you learn some of the hard truths about the publishing business. Publishers like emerging authors to prove themselves before investing large amounts in advances and other contractual payments. And you are not going to win all that you want at the outset.

Nevertheless you can and should make sure that all payments are governed by a written agreement, which includes not only the amount or percentage of money payable but also the timing of payments. A few unscrupulous publishers have been known to renege on their payments and leave authors and illustrators in the lurch!

5

CONTRACTS

~

A contract with a publisher is a legal document that indicates an intention to produce a book within a prescribed period of time. It also sets out the conditions that govern the business relationship you are entering into as author or illustrator. Therefore you should look carefully at the contract you are offered before you sign.

You should not assume your work will be published until a contract is signed by both you and the publisher. Whether you are to be paid a fee or a royalty, you will need a contract to define the responsibilities and obligations of the publisher and yourself.

For the writer, being offered a contract and signing it does not mean that no further work is required. But it does mean that the publisher has faith that the project will culminate in a published book. For the illustrator, no work should begin until a contract—or a written agreement of some kind—has been agreed upon and signed.

For the lay person unacquainted with contract law, the language and provisions of a contract may seem quite inscrutable. Book publishing arrangements cover complex areas such as international sales, subsidiary rights, and multi-media rights, and it is almost impossible for beginning writers or illustrators to make sense of the provisions that govern such areas. Never sign a contract before you have had a chance to take it away and examine its provisions carefully. If you don't understand one or more of the clauses in the contract, consult a lawyer or other expert, preferably one well acquainted with the publishing industry. Not all lawyers familiar with contract law will have sufficient knowledge of publishing practice to give useful advice. And while expert advice might make sense to you, publishing realities might not jibe with that advice.

In Canada, The Writers Union of Canada (TWUC) offers a package for new writers that includes a sample contract and other information on getting published, available to members as well as non-members. It includes a booklet entitled *Help Yourself to a Better Contract* and another titled *Model Trade Book Agreement*. In addition, the Union retains the services of a lawyer who can be consulted by writers who want detailed advice. But just because TWUC provides advice along with the generic contract doesn't mean that your publishers will agree to all your contract requests. For information on magazine contracts, contact the Professional Writers Association of Canada (PWAC).

> "WHETHER YOU ARE TO BE PAID A FEE OR A ROYALTY, YOU WILL NEED A CONTRACT TO DEFINE THE RESPONSIBILITIES AND OBLIGATIONS OF THE PUBLISHER AND YOURSELF."

In the US, advice on contracts is similarly available from the National Writers Union (NWU) and Society of Children's Book Writers and Illustrators (SCBWI). Contract tips are also available from the Author's Guild, and the American Society of Journalists and Authors (ASJA).

Note that electronic publishing now calls for a whole new set of contract considerations, including the definition of what are called "moral rights." Before a picture book can be adapted to a digital format, for example, the writer and illustrator have to agree to waive their moral rights so that words and pictures can be manipulated electronically.

6

SHOULD YOU GET AN AGENT?

~

Generally, most beginning writers and illustrators need to rely on their own energy and initiative to make contacts with publishers and conclude agreements with them. This calls for a good deal of legwork, research, and self-education in the workings of the publishing industry, as has already been indicated.

By the time a writer or illustrator has established a reputation through the publication of one or more books, it *may* seem best to hire an agent, particularly when it comes to dealing with foreign publishers. The agent is responsible for "placing" manuscripts with publishing houses that are most likely to want them, and for promoting the work of a writer or illustrator throughout the publishing industry. An agent also represents clients in the drawing up of contracts. In return the agent receives a percentage of the author's or illustrator's royalty. A good agent will also provide editorial input on the manuscripts she is trying to place.

> "THE AGENT IS RESPONSIBLE FOR 'PLACING' MANUSCRIPTS WITH PUBLISHING HOUSES THAT ARE MOST LIKELY TO WANT THEM, AND FOR PROMOTING THE WORK OF A WRITER OR ILLUSTRATOR THROUGHOUT THE PUBLISHING INDUSTRY."

Many established writers and illustrators in Canada do not have agents and continue to handle all their own business arrangements. In that way they feel they are more firmly in control of their professional lives (and are not paying out part of their income to someone else). Children's authors and illustrators particularly have felt that not many agents have sufficient knowledge of the children's publishing field to justify granting them a share of royalties. But the world is changing here, as in so many other aspects of the book industry. In the past several years, more agents are devoting themselves to the children's book business exclusively, developing their knowledge of the field. In response, some newer authors and illustrators and some well-established figures in the field have hired agents to handle their business affairs. As globalization affects the book industry, creative people have seen the value in engaging professional advisers to drum up projects in other countries, to handle foreign contracts and foreign rights sales.

Agents are not likely to be interested in representing hitherto unpublished writers or illustrators, since the odds against getting a publishing contract are very high and agents only receive their financial reward from published books. But there are exceptions, and from time to time agents do look at promising new writers and illustrators who they think might have significant careers.

Most major publishers in the United States do not accept unsolicited manuscripts; they only deal with manuscripts that come through agents. To some extent, the practice is also spreading to Canada. More than one major children's publisher has now said that it would only deal with agents and would no longer look at unsolicited manuscripts. Such changes in policy come about so that publishers can stem the flood of unsolicited material flowing into their offices. It may be that more publishers will follow this

"MORE THAN ONE MAJOR CHILDREN'S PUBLISHER HAS NOW SAID THAT IT WOULD ONLY DEAL WITH AGENTS AND WOULD NO LONGER LOOK AT UNSOLICITED MANUSCRIPTS."

path, so you need to keep in touch with writers' organizations in your region, The Writers Union of Canada (TWUC), the Canadian Society of Authors, Illustrators and Performers (CANSCAIP), or the Society of Children's Book Writers and Illustrators (SCBWI) to find out about further developments.

A final note here: just because someone calls himself an agent doesn't guarantee that he has the experience needed to represent you. As always, buyer beware.

7

THE NEW TECHNOLOGY

~

The publishing industry, like any other, has been affected by immense changes in technology. The book production process has altered startlingly in the past twenty years, and whole areas of expertise now no longer exist as new equipment and techniques have taken over and created new specializations.

Those who speculate about the future wonder about the continuing existence of books themselves, for a number of reasons. The growing sophistication of digitization is seen by some observers as a real threat to the book as we have known it. Children are learning to read on screens of various sorts and sizes, rather than by turning pages. And of course the continuing rise in paper prices can be seen as a warning about the resources on which the pulp and paper industry is founded. Those who have grown up in the publishing world of the past twenty years and more shake their heads and wonder about some of the more radical pronouncements about the disappearance of that precious artifact, the book.

Yet the most explosive event in book publishing at the turn of the new century, it could be said, was not a groundbreaking technological marvel, but the worldwide success of a children's book series, the adventures of an appealing English school boy, Harry Potter. The phenomenon dramatized by millions of *Harry Potter* book sales is a comforting one for traditional publishers. It informed many millions about the energy of the children's book world. It demonstrated that young readers were quite ready to put aside their Xboxes, computers, and other electronic diversions in order to read a good book—even a book of more than 700 pages. There is obviously a future in the technology of the ebook—but *Harry Potter* reminded us that a good book in traditional format still has enormous appeal. And it is even more reassuring that *Harry Potter* has not been the only series to attract millions of readers. Think Philip Pullman, at the upscale end of the spectrum, Stephanie Meyer for vampire yarns, and Lemony Snicket for the witty and macabre elements.

There have been enough dire predictions about the death of the book over the past five or six decades that this current one should be taken with a grain of salt. No matter the format, there will always be room for creators of wonderful stories to engage young readers, and for the visual artists who can enhance these stories by making them jump off the page—or the screen. What seems to be inevitable is that creators do need to be more and more aware of the business of getting their words and images out into the world; whether they want to or not, they need to be more conversant with various modes of publication, and how to find the one that suits their work best. And when it comes to encountering the actual reader, it's already been demonstrated that the children's writer and illustrator can make a life-changing impact on the reading lives of their audiences—but that's another story.

"THERE IS OBVIOUSLY A FUTURE IN THE TECHNOLOGY OF THE EBOOK—BUT *HARRY POTTER* REMINDED US THAT A GOOD BOOK IN TRADITIONAL FORMAT STILL HAS ENORMOUS APPEAL."

8

ORGANIZATIONS

~

A number of organizations provide useful information and resources for writers, illustrators, and others interested in children's books.

For Information About Canadian Children's Books:

The Canadian Children's Book Centre
Suite 101, 40 Orchard View Blvd., Toronto, ON M4R 1B9
Phone: (416) 975-0010 Fax: (416) 975-8970
info@bookcentre.ca; www.bookcentre.ca

The Canadian Children's Book Centre is a non-profit organization established to promote the reading, writing, and illustrating of Canadian children's books. It sponsors the annual Children's Book Week, provides reference services, and has an extensive publications program for teachers, librarians, booksellers, parents—and children. Those interested in learning about the Centre's services can make contact by phone, fax, mail, or in person.

Communication-Jeunesse
1685, rue Fleury Est, Bureau 200, Montréal, Québec H2C 1T1
Phone: (514) 286-6020 Fax: (514) 286-6093
com.jeunesse@videotron.ca; www.communication-jeunesse.qc.ca

Communication-Jeunesse is a non-profit organization devoted to the promotion of Quebec books in French for young people. It provides information, organizes reading activities in schools, and promotes quality publishing for children in the province.

For Information About Children's Books in the United States:

The Children's Book Council
54 West 39th Street, 14th floor, New York, NY 10018
Phone: (212) 966-1990 Fax: (212) 966-2073
cbc.info@cbcbooks.org; www.cbcbooks.org

The Children's Book Council is the national non-profit trade association for children's trade book publishers. The CBC offers children's publishers the opportunity to work together on issues of importance to the industry at large, including educational programming, literacy advocacy, and collaborations with other national organizations. Members span the spectrum from large international houses to smaller independent presses. Membership in the CBC is open to US publishers of children's trade books and industry-affiliated companies.

The Center for Children's Books (CCB)
Graduate School of Library and Information Science
University of Illinois at Urbana-Champaign
501 E. Daniel St., Champaign, IL 61820
Phone: (217) 244-9331 Fax: (217) 333-5603
ccb@illinois.edu; http://ccb.lis.illinois.edu

The Center for Children's Books (CCB) at the Graduate School of Library and Information Science (GSLIS) is a crossroads for critical inquiry, professional training, and educational outreach related to youth-focused resources, literature and librarianship. The Center's mission is to facilitate the creation and dissemination of exemplary and progressive research and scholarship related to all aspects of children's and young adult literature; media and resources for young (age 0-18) audiences; and youth services librarianship.

The Bulletin of the Center for Children's Books (an affiliate of The Center for Children's Books)

Editorial Offices: Graduate School of Library and Information Science

501 E. Daniel St., MC-493, Champaign, Illinois 61820-6211

Phone: (217) 244-0324 Fax: (217) 224-3302

bccb@illinois.edu; http://bccb.lis.illinois.edu/

Cooperative Children's Book Center

School of Education

University of Wisconsin-Madison

600 North Park Street, Room 4290, Madison, Wisconsin 53706

Phone: (608) 263-3720 Fax: (608) 262-4933

www.education.wisc.edu/ccbc/

The Cooperative Children's Book Center (CCBC) is a unique examination, study and research library of the School of Education at the University of Wisconsin-Madison. The CCBC's non-circulating collections include current, retrospective, and historical books published for children and young adults.

For a **directory of authors**, see http://www.kidsreads.com/authors/authors.asp

ASSOCIATIONS

The following associations are open to professional (published) as well as non-professional (unpublished) writers and illustrators. They provide various services, publications, information, and programs for their members.

IN CANADA

CANSCAIP

(The Canadian Society of Children's Authors, Illustrators, and Performers)
104-40 Orchard View Blvd., Lower Level Entrance, Toronto, ON M4R 1B9
office@canscaip.org; www.canscaip.org

CANSCAIP offers support, information (through its quarterly newsletter, *CANSCAIP News*), and an opportunity to meet with professional members. Regular monthly meetings are held in Toronto and regional meetings occur from time to time in other parts of the country. Manuscript evaluations can also be arranged through CANSCAIP. More information is available through regional representatives.

Canadian Authors Association

National Office:
74 Mississauga St. East, Orillia, ON, L3V 1V5
Phone: (705) 653-0323 Toll-free: (866) 216-6222
admin@canauthors.org;www.canauthors.org

One of the oldest established writers organizations in Canada, the CAA has provincial and regional branches across the country, each of which runs regular meetings throughout the year.

The Writers' Trust of Canada

90 Richmond Street East, Suite 200, Toronto, Ontario M5C 1P1
Phone: (416) 504-8222 Fax (416) 504-9090
info@writerstrust.com; www.writerstrust.com

The Writers' Trust is an association that has, over many years, planned many events that bring together authors and readers. It is also the administrator (since 2003) of the Vicky Metcalf Award for Children's Literature.

Provincial Writers Associations

Provincial writers' associations offer information, advice, workshops, and other services for professional and non-professional members.

Association des auteures et auteurs de l'Ontario français
335-B, rue Cumberland, Ottawa, Ontario K1N 7J3
Phone: (613) 744-0902 Fax: (613) 744-6915
dg.aaof@franco.ca; http://aaof.ca/

Writers' Alliance of Newfoundland and Labrador
Haymarket Square 202-223 Duckworth St., St. John's, NL, A1C 6N1
Phone: (709) 739-5215
Toll free: (866) 739-5215
Fax: (709) 739-5931
http://wanl.ca

PEI Writers' Guild
Phone: (902) 892-9788
peiwritersguild@gmail.com; http://www.peiwritersguild.com/
Blog: http://peiwritersguild.wordpress.com/

Writers' Federation of Nova Scotia
1113 Marginal Road, Halifax, NS B3H 4P7
Phone: (902) 423-8116 Fax: (902) 422-0881
talk@writers.ns.ca; http://www.writers.ns.ca/

Writers' Federation of New Brunswick
P.O. Box 306, Moncton, NB E1C 8L4

Fax: (506) 459-7228

wfnb@nb.aibn.com; http://www.umce.ca/wfnb/

Quebec Writers' Federation (QWF)

1200 Atwater Ave, Westmount, QC H3Z 1X4

Phone: (514) 933-0878

www.qwf.org/

Union des écrivaines et des écrivains québécois (UNEQ)

3492, avenue Laval, Montréal, QC H2X 3C8

Phone: (514) 849-8540 Fax: (514) 849-6239

ecrivez@uneq.qc.ca; www.uneq.qc.ca/

Manitoba Writers' Guild Inc.

218-100 Arthur Street, Winnipeg, MB R3B 1H3

Phone: (204) 944-8013

ibindi@mbwriter.mb.ca; www.mbwriter.mb.ca/

Saskatchewan Writers' Guild (SWG)

Box 3986, Regina, SK S4P 3R9

info@skwriter.com; www.skwriter.com

Writers Guild of Alberta

Head Office:

Percy Page Centre, 11759 Groat Road, Edmonton, AB T5M 3K6

Phone: (780) 422-8174 or (800) 665-5354 Fax: (780) 422-2663

mail@writersguild.ab.ca; www.writersguild.ab.ca/

Southern Alberta Office:

Lord Denning House, 509, 20th Avenue SW, Calgary, AB   T2S 0E7

Phone: (403) 265-2226 Fax: (403) 234-9532

Federation of BC Writers

Box 3887, Station Terminal, Vancouver, BC V6B 3Z3

Fax: (604) 683-8269

bcwritersfed@gmail.com; http://bcwriters.com

Children's Writers and Illustrators of British Columbia Society (CWILL BC)
1256 Oliver Street, Victoria, BC V85 4W9
membership@cwill.bc.ca; http://www.cwill.bc.ca/
Blog: http://cwillbc.wordpress.com/

IN THE UNITED STATES

For a complete listing of US state writing associations, go to www.squidoo.com/localwritersassociationsbystate

PROFESSIONAL ASSOCIATIONS

The following professional associations provide services for professional writers and editors.

IN CANADA

The Book and Periodical Council
Suite 107, 192 Spadina Avenue, Toronto, Ontario M5T 2C2
Phone: (416) 975-9366 Fax: (416) 975-1839
info@thebpc.ca; http://www.thebpc.ca/

The Book and Periodical Council is an umbrella organization of professional associations that encompass the entire book industry in Canada—writers, editors, publishers, booksellers, wholesalers, and librarians.

Editors' Association of Canada (EAC)
502-27 Carlton St., Toronto, Ontario M5B 1L2
Phone: (416) 975-1379 Toll-free: (866) 226-3348 Fax: (416) 975-1637
info@editors.ca; www.editors.ca

EAC was founded in 1979 and now has a membership of more than 1,000 professional and associate members across Canada. Membership meetings and workshops are held regularly in British Columbia, Toronto, the National Capital Region, and Montreal.

The League of Canadian Poets

312 - 192 Spadina Avenue, Toronto, ON M5T 2C2
Phone: (416) 504-1657 Fax: (416) 504-0096
admin@poets.ca; http://poets.ca

The League of Canadian Poets provides a touring program, funded by the Canada Council, which takes published poets into schools and libraries across Canada.

Professional Writers Association of Canada (PWAC)

215 Spadina Avenue, Suite 123, Toronto, Ontario M5T 2C7
Phone: (416) 504-1645 Fax: (416) 913-2327
info@pwac.ca; www.pwac.ca

PWAC offers information to professional members—and also to aspiring magazine writers who need to know about fees, contracts, and copyright matters.

Playwrights Guild of Canada

215 Spadina Ave., Suite 210, Toronto, Ontario M5T 2C7
info@playwrightsguild.ca; www.playwrightsguild.ca/pgc/

The Playwrights Guild's publishing program includes plays for young people, as well as works designed for the adult audience. Advice and information is available to aspiring playwrights whose work has not yet been produced or published.

The Writers' Union of Canada (TWUC)

90 Richmond Street East, Suite 200, Toronto, ON M5C 1P1
Phone: (416) 703-8982 Fax: (416) 504-9090
info@writersunion.ca; www.writersunion.ca

TWUC offers legal advice and information about all aspects of the writing business in Canada to members and non-members. To qualify for membership, a writer must have at least one title published professionally; self-published books are not eligible. TWUC's website (www.writersunion.ca) provides links to many other literary organizations in Canada (click on Literary Links).

IN THE UNITED STATES

Editorial Freelancers Association (EFA)
71 West 23rd Street, 4th Floor, New York, NY 10010-4102
Phone: (212) 929-5400 Fax: (212) 929-5439
office@the-efa.org; http://www.the-efa.org/

The Academy of American Poets
75 Maiden Lane, Suite 901, New York, NY 10038
Phone: (212) 274-0343 Fax: (212) 274-9427
academy@poets.org; www.poets.org/

The Academy is a non-profit organization with a mission to support American poets at all stages of their careers and to foster the appreciation of contemporary poetry.

Poetry Society of America
15 Gramercy Park, New York, New York 10003
Phone: (212) 254-9628 Fax: (212) 673-2352
www.poetrysociety.org/

The Poetry Society of America, the oldest poetry organization in the country, has established important awards for poets at all stages of their careers, and there was from the earliest days a particular emphasis on welcoming the new.

Poets & Writers
National Office:
90 Broad Street, Suite 2100, New York, NY 10004
Phone: (212) 226-3586 Fax: (212) 226-3963
admin@pw.org

California Office:
2035 Westwood Boulevard, Suite 211, Los Angeles, CA 90025
Phone: (310) 481-7195 Fax: (310) 481-7193
calif@pw.org; www.pw.org/

P&W publishes *Poets & Writers Magazine*, and is a supporter of emerging writers.

American Society of Journalists and Authors (ASJA)
1501 Broadway, Suite 403, New York, NY 10036
Phone: (212) 997-0947 Fax: (212) 937-2315
http://www.asja.org

The Dramatists Guild of America
1501 Broadway, Suite 701, New York, NY 10036
Phone: (212) 398-9366 Fax: (212) 944-0420
www.dramatistsguild.com/

The Dramatists Guild of America was established over eighty years ago, and is the only professional association which advances the interests of playwrights, composers, lyricists and librettists writing for the living stage. The Guild has over 6,000 members nationwide, from beginning writers to the most prominent authors represented on Broadway, Off-Broadway and in regional theaters.

National Writers Union
National Office: 256 West 38th Street, Suite 703, New York, NY 10018
Phone: (212) 254-0279 Fax: (212) 254-0673
nwu@nwu.org; http://www.nwu.org/

The National Writers Union UAW Local 1981 is the only labor union that represents freelance writers.

⑨

GOVERNMENT CULTURAL PROGRAMS AND GRANTS

~

IN CANADA

Up to the early 1990s, several provincial and federal agencies provided funding for aspiring and professional writers through a variety of programs, in addition to block grants for Canadian-owned publishing houses. Severe funding cutbacks in government support to the arts started hitting in the mid-1990s, so that while cultural funding programs still existed on paper, some were no longer operative due to the scale of the cutbacks. Recently some of these programs have been restored or reactivated.

News of recent developments in these programs is available through provincial writers' associations and through The Writers Union of Canada website. Aspirants can also contact the Canada Council directly.

The Canada Council for the Arts
Writing & Publishing Section
350 Albert Street, PO Box 1047, Ottawa, Ontario K1P 5V8
Phone: (613) 566-4414 Toll-free: (800) 263-5588 Fax: (613) 566-4390
www.canadacouncil.ca

IN THE UNITED STATES

National Endowment for the Arts

1100 Pennsylvania Avenue, NW, Washington, DC 20506-0001
Phone: (202) 682-5400 Voice/T.T.Y.: (202) 682-5496
webmgr@arts.endow.gov; http://www.arts.gov/

The National Endowment for the Arts was established by Congress in 1965 as an independent agency of the Federal Government. To date, the NEA has awarded more than $4 billion to support artistic excellence, creativity, and innovation for the benefit of individuals and communities. The NEA extends its work through partnerships with state arts agencies, local leaders, other federal agencies, and the philanthropic sector.

10

RESOURCES

BOOKS ON WRITING IN GENERAL, AND CHILDREN'S WRITING IN PARTICULAR

~

Many books that illuminate the field of children's writing and illustrating. Most of them should be available in the local branch of your public library, or can be ordered through your bookseller. The field covered is broad—from practical guides on how to get published to more personal encouragements on getting the creative juices flowing. Some of the titles focus particularly on children's writing; others deal with writing and the creative process in general.

Aitken, Joan. *The Way to Write for Children*. Elm Tree Books, 1982.

Allen, Roberta. *Fast Fiction: Creating Fiction in Five Minutes*. Story Press, 1997.

Archbold, Rick, Doug Gibson, Dennis Lee, John Pearce, Jan Walter. *Author & Editor, A Working Guide*. Prentice-Hall, 1983.

Bernays, Anne, and Pamela Painter. *What If?: Writing Exercises for Fiction Writers*. Rev. ed. Longman, 2000.

Bicknell, Treld, and Felicity Trotman. *How to Write and Illustrate Children's Books and Get Them Published*. Macdonald Orbis, 1988

Booth, David. *Writers on Writing: Guide to Writing and Illustrating Children's Books*. Overlea House, 1989.

Browne, Renni, and Dave King. *Self-editing for Fiction Writers*. HarperCollins, 1993.

Cameron, Julia and Mark Bryan. *The Artist's Way: A Spiritual Path to Higher Creativity*. Putnam's, 1992.

Card, Orson Scott. *Characters & Viewpoint*. Writer's Digest, 1988.

Cooper, Susan. *Dreams and Wishes: Essays on Writing for Children*. Margaret K. McElderry Books, 1996.

Dibell, Anson. *Elements of Writing Fiction: Plot*. Writer's Digest, 1988.

Ellis, Sarah. *The Young Writer's Companion*. Groundwood, 1999.

Fitz-Randolph, Jane. *How to Write for Children and Young Adults: A Handbook*. Rev. ed. Johnson Books, 1987.

Fox, Mem. *Dear Mem Fox, I Have Read All Your Books, Even the Pathetic Ones*. Harcourt Brace Jovanovich, 1990.

Friedman, Bonnie. *Writing Past Dark: Envy, Fear, Distraction and Other Dilemmas in the Writer's Life*. HarperCollins, 1993.

Fritz, Jean, and William Zinsser. *Worlds of Childhood: The Art and Craft of Writing for Children*. Houghton Mifflin, 1990.

Fulford, Robert. *The Triumph of Narrative*. Anansi, 1999.

Gardner, John. *The Art of Fiction*. Alfred A. Knopf, 1984.

Goldberg, Natalie. *Wild Mind*. Bantam Books, 1990.

Goldberg, Natalie. *Writing Down the Bones*. Random House, 1986.

Gould, June. *The Writer in All of Us: Improving Your Writing Through Childhood Memories*. E.P. Dutton, 1989.

Grant, Janet E. *Young Person's Guide to Becoming a Writer*. Betterway Publications, 1991.

Hemley, Robin. *Turning Life Into Fiction*. Story Press, 1994.

Hodgins, Jack. *A Passion for Narrative*. McClelland & Stewart, 1993.

Hunter, Mollie. *Talent is Not Enough: Mollie Hunter on Writing for Children*. Harper & Row, 1976.

Irwin, Hadley, and Jeanette Eyerly. *Writing Young Adult Novels*. Writer's Digest, 1988.

King, Stephen. *On Writing*. Scribner, 2000.

Krailing, Tessa. *How to Write for Children*. Allison & Busby, 1988.

Lamotte, Anne. *Bird by Bird: Some Instructions on Writing and Life*. Pantheon, 1994.

Lewis, Claudia. *Writing for Young Children*. Rev. ed. Penguin Books, 1982.

Litowinsky, Olga. *Writing and Publishing Books for Children in the 1990s: The Inside Story from the Editor's Desk*. Walker, 1992.

Maugham, W. Somerset. *A Writer's Notebook*. Heineman, 1951.

Novakovich, Josip. *Fiction Writer's Workshop*. Story Press, 1995.

Rainer, Tristine. *The New Diary: How to Use a Journal for Self Guidance and Expanded Creativity*. St. Martin's Press, 1978.

Ray, Robert J. *The Weekend Novelist*. Dell, 1994.

Reidel, Kate. *Signposts—A Guide to Self-Publishing*. Book and Periodical Council, 1992. (Available through the Book and Periodical Council, Ste. 107, 192 Spadina Avenue, Toronto, Ontario M5T 2C2.)

Roberts, Ellen E.M. *The Children's Picture Book: How to Write It, How to Sell It*. Writer's Digest Books, 1986.

Roberts, Ellen E.M. *Non-fiction for Children: How to Write It, How to Sell It*. Writer's Digest Books, 1986.

Scofield, Sandra. *The Scene Book*. Penguin, 2007

Seger, Linda. *Creating Unforgettable Characters*. Henry Holt & Co., 1990.

Seuling, Barbara. *How to Write a Children's Book and Get It Published*. Scribner, 1984.

Shulevitz, Uri. *Writing with Pictures: How to Write and Illustrate Children's Books*. Watson-Guptill, 1985.

Stinson, Kathy. *Writing Picture Books—What Works and What Doesn't*. Pembroke Press, 1992.

Stinson, Kathy. *Writing Your Best Picture Book Ever*. Pembroke Press, 1994.

Strunk, William Jr., and E.B. White. *The Elements of Style, 50ᵗʰ Anniversary Edition*. Simon and Shuster, 2009.

Tomajczyk, S.F. *The Children's Writer's Marketplace*. Running Press, 1987.

Woolley, Catherine. *Writing for Children*. New American Library, 1990.

Wyndham, Lee, and Arnold Madison. *Writing for Children and Teenagers*. Rev. 3rd ed. Writer's Digest Books, 1988.

Yolen, Jane. *Writing Books for Children*. New ed. completely rev. and enlarged. The Writer, 1983.

BOOKS — ILLUSTRATION

Arisman, Marshall, and Steven Heller. *Marketing Illustration: New Venues, New Styles, New Methods*. Allworth Press, 2009.

BOOKS — COMMENTARIES ON CHILDREN'S LITERATURE

These titles provide commentaries or overviews on children's literature.

Baker, Deirdre, and Ken Setterington. *A Guide to Canadian Children's Books*. McClelland and Stewart, 2003.

Carpenter, Humphrey, and Mari Prichard. *The Oxford Companion to Children's Literature*. Oxford, 1999.

Edwards, Gail, and Judith Saltman. *Picturing Canada: A History of Canadian Children's Illustrated Books and Publishing*. University of Toronto Press, 2010.

Egoff, Sheila, and Judith Saltman. *The New Republic of Childhood: A Critical Guide to Canadian Children's Literature in English*. Oxford, 1990.

Landsberg, Michele. *Michele Landsberg's Guide to Children's Books*. Penguin Books, 1985.

Lukens, Rebecca. *A Critical Handbook of Children's Literature*. 3rd ed. Scott, Foresman, 1986.

Lurie, Alison. *Don't Tell the Grown-ups: Why Kids Love the Books They Do*. Little, Brown, 1990.

Paterson, Katherine. *Gates of Excellence: On Reading and Writing Books for Children*. Elsevier/Nelson Books, 1981.

Paterson, Katherine. *The Spying Heart: More Thoughts on Reading and Writing Books for Children*. Lodestar Books, 1989.

Rae, Arlene Perley. *Everybody's Favourites: Canadians Talk About Books that Changed Their Lives*. Viking Penguin, 1997.

PERIODICALS

~

IN CANADA

Jeunesse: Young People, Texts, Cultures. Centre for Research in Young People's Texts and Cultures, University of Winnipeg. http://jeunessejournal.ca

Children's Choices of Canadian Books. Citizens' Committee on Children, Ottawa.

CM Magazine—www.umanitoba.ca/cm (online only)

Emergency Librarian. Dyad Services, Vancouver.

The Looking Glass—www.the-looking-glass.net (online only)

Quill & Quire. Key Publishers, Toronto. (includes monthly section entitled *Books for Young People.*) www.quillandquire.com

Resource Links. Rockland Press, Vancouver. www.resourcelinksmagazine.ca

The Teaching Librarian. Ontario Library Association, Toronto. http://www.accessola.com/osla/bins/content_page. asp?cid=1488&lang=1

There is a wonderful variety of websites devoted to children's books available on the Internet. For more resources, go to The Canadian Children's Book Centre's website—www.bookcentre.ca—and click through to Talk About Books, Journals and Publications.

IN THE UNITED STATES

Publishers Weekly has a children's section (has print and digital editions)
www.publishersweekly.com/pw/by-topic/childrens/index.html

Bookmark (New York State Library)
http://www.amazon.com/Bookmarks/dp/B0000AJLX9

Reads over 500 book reviews a month.

The Horn Book Magazine
http://www.hbook.com/magazine

The Horn Book Guide to Children's and Young Adult Books.
www.hbook.com/guide/

Each semi-annual issue of the print Horn Book Guide rates and reviews over 2,000 titles—virtually every children's and young adult book published in the US in a six-month period.

The Alan Review (Assembly On Literature For Adolescents)
www.alan-ya.org/the-alan-review/

The journal contains articles on YA literature and its teaching, interviews with authors, reports on publishing trends, current research on YA literature, and a section of reviews of new books.

Bookbird: A Journal of International Children's Literature
http://www.ibby.org/index.php?id=1035

Bookbird aims to communicate new ideas to the whole community of readers interested in children's books.

Booklist http://www.ala.org/ala/aboutala/offices/publishing
booklist_publications/booklist/booklist.cfm

Published by the American Library Association, Booklist magazine delivers over 8,000 recommended-only reviews of books, audiobooks, reference sources, video, and DVD titles each year.

Journal of Children's Literature (Children's Literature Assembly)
http://www.childrensliteratureassembly.org/

Contains articles by noted authors, profiles of authors and illustrators, research updates, and reviews of children's and professional books to broaden your knowledge about children's literature.

The Five Owls
http://www.fiveowls.com/

The Five Owls is a quarterly publication devoted to the field of children's literature.

Kirkus Reviews: Children's and Young Adult Edition
http://www.kirkusreviews.com/book-reviews/childrens-books/

Founded in 1933, *Kirkus* reviews more than 500 pre-publication books each month, including fiction, nonfiction, children's, and young-adult books.

The Lion and The Unicorn: A Critical Journal of Children's Literature
http://www.press.jhu.edu/journals/lion_and_the_unicorn/

An international theme- and genre-centered journal committed to a serious, ongoing discussion of literature for children.

Sankofa: A Journal of African Children's and Young Adult Literature
http://grizzly.morgan.edu/~english/sankofa/index.html

Provides readers with in-depth book reviews and scholarly articles on emerging trends in African and African diaspora literatures.

School Library Journal
http://www.schoollibraryjournal.com/

The world's largest reviewer of children's and young adult content—principally books, but also audio, video, and the Web.

Voya: Voice of Youth Advocates
http://www.voya.com/

VOYA is a bimonthly journal devoted exclusively to the informational needs of teenagers.

Other journal information/listings can be found at: http://ion.uwinnipeg.ca/~nodelman/resources/journals.htm

OTHERS

Children's Writer's & Illustrator's Market

Covers articles and interviews with publishing professionals, from first-time authors to seasoned editors. www.cwim.com/

Children's Writer: Newsletter of Writing and Publishing Trends www.childrenswriter.com

A monthly publication providing information and views on what's current in children's publishing.

ON PUBLISHING FOR CHILDREN

Book Marketing and Book Promotion: Creating Worldwide Bestsellers http://www.bookmarket.com/childrens.htm

An online guide on how to submit to publishers, specifically children's publishers.

AFTERWORD

~

Being a writer or an artist is usually a lifelong obsession. Once infected by the habit, you probably have it forever.

And the obsession is a lonely one. It requires hours of solitary practice, as you hone your skills and create the images in words and pictures that mean so much to you. For the writer or artist, the hours alone can be exciting and exhilarating because they are the focus of your creativity.

It's important, though, to emerge from your office or studio from time to time, to breathe fresh air, to find new stimulation, to re-acquaint yourself with the world. It can also be important to become part of a network of individuals with similar inclinations. Writers or illustrators for children are sometimes treated as if they are children, still unformed. "When are you going to be ready to write for adults?" is a refrain too often heard by even the most accomplished in the field. It's enormously reassuring, therefore, to find others who are just as enthusiastic and committed as you are, whether it's through CANSCAIP or SCBWI, a children's literature course at your local university or community college, a writers' group you have helped form yourself, or through the many workshops and conferences across Canada and the United States whose focus is the creation and study of children's literature.

As you create manuscripts and illustrations, it is through the network that you can sound out your ideas and your first attempts. The network can also function as an information exchange, a means of plugging into the market and keeping up to date with publishers' needs and interests.

Even when you have your foot in the door and have published

your first book, the network remains just as important as a way of extending your associations with others in the industry—authors, illustrators, publishers, editors, designers, as well as the librarians and teachers and parents who are looking for new books on themes still unexplored.

The world of children's books is one of the most exciting and satisfying fields available to the creative spirit. Whether you are reader, writer, or illustrator, you will find a lifetime of stimulation through the books aimed at young readers. Write on!

ACKNOWLEDGMENTS

~

This guide is based on more than twenty-five years experience teaching adults who want to write for children and almost thirty-five years working as in-house and freelance editor for a number of Canadian publishers.

When I worked at The Canadian Children's Book Centre in Toronto in the 1980s, a steady flow of individuals arrived on our doorstep who felt they had created the great Canadian children's story but didn't know how to get it published. Fledgling writers and budding illustrators asked for advice and direction in their search for publishing success.

In 1984, in response, the Centre launched a series of month-long courses in Writing for Children. The four weekly meetings in each course allowed us to provide basic information about the children's publishing industry as well as suggestions about how one might approach a publisher with a manuscript. But time constraints meant there was only a limited opportunity to workshop students' writing.

In the fall of 1986, I began teaching a ten-week course in Writing for Children for George Brown College's Continuing Education division. A year later a second workshop was added to accommodate those who wanted to return to the program to continue with the process we'd set up—in effect to establish an ongoing children's writers' workshop. It is to those who have been with me in the George Brown Advanced Writing for Children workshop—some staying with it for more than ten years—that I owe so much, both for the ideas and inspiration for this guide. It is in working with them that I have come to understand the passion, the practical difficulties, and the real struggles experienced by writers who are trying to break into the children's book industry.

In the early years of the Writing for Children program, the success of the course fed a series of annual weekend conferences staged in Toronto during the summer months, entitled *Storymakers*. The five *Storymakers* conferences were exhilarating creative gatherings, attended by hundreds of eager writers, and fed by the contributions of dozens of the most talented of children's authors, illustrators, and editors.

Since September 1989, George Brown's Writing for Children courses have been taught at Mabel's Fables, a thriving children's bookstore in mid-town Toronto. My thanks to the store's original proprietors, Susan McCullough and her sister Eleanor LeFave, who so generously made available their space for our meetings. At various times, sections of the course have also been taught at the Casa Loma campus of George Brown, and at the North York Central Library; writers in these venues also contributed to the knowledge base this guide draws from.

Since the inauguration of the Writing for Children program at George Brown College, I have also been asked to give writing workshops in Nanaimo, Vancouver, Edmonton, Regina, Saskatoon, Winnipeg, Montreal, Halifax, and St. John's. In each place, I was as much learner as teacher. In addition, Kathy Stinson and I have, since 2006, offered a week-long writing workshop at our summer home on the south shore of Nova Scotia—an experience that has informed and refined our views of the kind of insight and direction writers most benefit from. In Kathy's career as a skilled and versatile writer of all genres of books for young readers, I have found a great deal of inspiration. Also, in recent years, author Ted Staunton has shared the instructor's role at George Brown with me, and his advice and experience have been invaluable.

Many writers, published and unpublished, have shared their wisdom with me over the years, too many to be named and given their due. I do need to thank Heather Collins who explained to me the rigors of finding work as an illustrator. Also thanks to Rob Morphy who has provided web links for various organizations and resources. I also want to acknowledge Brian Doyle, a great teacher and a lyrical and uncompromisingly honest writer, much celebrated in Canada and beyond, who was my close colleague teaching high-school English in Ottawa in the heady sixties and seventies, whose encouragement and advice has always been available, offered discreetly and generously, and whose fifty-year friendship is an incalculable boon.

Lastly, I must acknowledge my debt to Peggy Needham, inspired and devoted faculty adviser at George Brown College until her retirement in the summer of 2000, a friend and supporter since the beginning of this enterprise. Very little of this would have been possible without her help.

INDEX

~

A

Access Copyright, 85
agents, 92-93
associations, 99-105
See also organizations
audience, 34, 39

B

bookstores, 4, 41, 42
Bourgeois, Paulette, 48, 57

C

children's literature, 4-6, 26-28
commissioned work, 47
contracts, 90-91
copyright, 83-86
Copyright Clearance Center, 85
The Copyright Office, 84

D

digital technology, 85, 94-95
    See also electronic media
Dorling Kindersley, 63
Doyle, Brian, 14, 35
drama, 31, 41

E

easy readers, 26-27
editors, 37, 56-58
educational publishing, 41-42
illustrating, 67-68
electronic media, 5, 85, 91, 94-95
Ellis, Sarah, 35
Eyvindson, Peter, 12-13

F

fee payments, 87, 88-89
feedback, 37
fiction, 26-30
first chapter books, 26-27
first draft, 35-36

G

genres, 21
government programs and grants, 106-7

H

Harry Potter, 94-95
Hesse, Karen, 31

I

ideas, 83
illustrating books, 23-24
    educational, 67-68
    non-fiction, 63-64
    picture books, 61-62, 72-74
illustrators, 23-24, 60, 61-62
    approaching publishers, 70-71
    freelancing, 75
    opportunities, 67-68
    portfolios, 69-71
    training, 65-66
    working on a book, 72-74
imagery, 14
Internet, 17, 85

J

juvenile novels, 27

K

Katz, Welwyn, 53

L

Lunn, Janet, 36

M

magazines, 43, 44
Mahy, Margaret, 52
manuscript submission, 24, 25, 33-34, 49
    guidelines, 49-51
    solicited manuscripts, 49
    unsolicited manuscripts, 47-48
markets, 20, 25-26, 27, 32
McClintock, Norah, 29-30
McFarlane, Leslie, 87
middle readers, 27

moral rights, 85, 91
Morphy, Rob, 43
Munsch, Bob, 48

N
non-fiction, 31-34
   illustrating, 63-64
notes, keeping, 14, 16, 35
novels, 26-30

O
online publishing, 44-45
online resources, 17, 28, 43
   See also resources
Oppel, Ken, 33
organizations, 13, 37, 96-98
   See also associations

P
payment, 87-89
picture books, 22, 23-26
   illustrating, 61-62, 72-74
plan, making a, 10-11, 29-30, 33-34
poetry, 30-31
publishing, 39, 40
   educational publishing, 41-42
   finding a publisher, 81-82
   production process, 78-80
   publishers, 24, 33-34, 41
   risks, 48
   self-publishing, 44-46
   trade books, 38-43
Pullman, Philip, 10-11

Q
quoting other works, 85-86

R
readers, young, 5-6, 14, 20, 26-28, 38
reading, 12-13
reading aloud, 33, 26-27
Reid, Barbara, 70-71
rejection, 52-54
resources, 108
   commentaries, 112
   on illustrating, 111

periodicals, 113-16
   on writing, 108-11
   See also online resources
revising See rewriting
rewriting, 30, 36
royalties, 87-89

S
school libraries, 42
self-publishing, 44-46
short stories, 28
Staunton, Ted, 19
story, 21-22, 29-30
support groups, 16-17

T
Taylor, Peter, 54
technology See electronic media
teen fiction See young adult novel
theater, children's, 31, 41
time for writing, 15-16
trade books, 44-43

U
US Copyright Office, 84

V
voice, 13, 14

W
workshops, 16-18
writer's block, 36
The Writers Union of Canada
(TWUC), 91
writing courses, 16-17
writing for children, 12, 19-20
   markets, 20, 25-26, 27, 32
writing methods, 29-30, 35-37
Wynne-Jones, Tim, 53

Y
young adult novel, 27-28